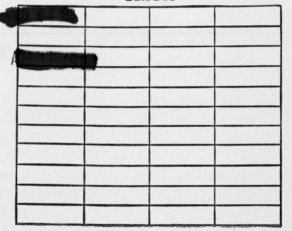

After the

After the

Conflict and Consensus

A Report on the
First American Congress of Theatre

By Stuart W. Little

ARNO
A NEW YORK TIMES COMPANY
NEW YORK   1975

ISBN: 0-405-06661-9

Contents

Statement of Purpose

The organizers of the First American Congress of Theatre (FACT) issued the following Statement of Purpose as the Congress convened in Princeton, New Jersey, on June 2, 1974:

Theatre in the United States has traditionally dealt with its problems individualistically, each producing unit fending for itself as best it could. Operating in this way, it has become a highly diversified, vital and innovative artistic force, respected and emulated throughout the world. But its economic viability has been made increasingly precarious by the familiar ills that beset the nation's social structure.

These problems have reached a point at which they can no longer be dealt with effectively by any one segment of the theatre. The entire community will have to decide as a unit what must be done to overcome the effects on attendance of urban deterioration, transportation problems, and the disastrous conjunction of inflation and economic recession.

It must consider the appropriate ways of dealing with rising costs which require ever longer runs and fuller houses to recoup production costs — making it ever more difficult to undertake venturesome productions.

It must reexamine its traditional marketing practices to determine what new and more imaginative avenues can be found to increase its box office revenues.

7

It must reexamine the sources of support to see what can be done to make its financing more reliable and less capricious.

With the set of common problems growing increasingly acute, it has become imperative that the various theatrical units, whatever their aesthetic affiliation or their administrative and financial structure, come together with all those interested in their welfare to determine what the theatre can do to help itself while maintaining its artistic integrity and traditional vitality.

This will be the subject of a National Theatre Conference which, for the first time, will bring together leaders from every sector of theatrical activity — the commercial, the regional, the experimental, the Black theatre, the foundations and the governmental arts organizations. This Conference will be a working enterprise whose objectives are to identify the problems and to design practical programs which American theatre can undertake. It will reflect the experience and knowledge of the entire spectrum of American theatre.

No group with a direct stake in the future of the theatre can afford to abstain from the process of reexamination of the premises of theatrical organization and operation which this Conference will launch. The issues are too important and the problems too pressing to permit postponement of common strategies for whose design this Conference will provide the forum.

I. What FACT Decided

For four days in June, 1974, 224 theatre professionals, foundation executives, educators, government officials, and others with a special interest in theatre met in Princeton, New Jersey, to discuss the problems, and the opportunities, facing American theatre. It was the first major theatrewide conference to be called in many years (the last comparable such meeting was held during the 1930's depression), and it was an unusual meeting, for any time or profession, in that it brought together so diverse and inclusive a group of dedicated experts.

The early June weather was fine throughout, favoring agreement even when, indoors, the discussions among participants holding strongly opposing viewpoints were spirited and occasionally stormy. At the end of its four days, the First American Congress of Theatre (FACT) had come through its debates and disagreements with a decision to continue in being as one organization that would represent as well as possible all sectors of American theatre.

No master plan for the American theatre was evolved; no convenient and neat resolution of the often conflicting opinions and ideas expressed would have been possible. Instead, the intangible benefits of FACT were ones of definition and changed outlook for the theatre. The Congress produced awareness and a recognition of new forces and formations operating within the theatre nationally. It ended with general agreement at least to explore ways to meet the shared uncertainties and problems of the future in a new spirit of cooperation and unity and to formulate plans for action.

The intention of the organizers of the Congress was to test the proposition – at the time, perhaps, merely a hope – that the theatre, broadly considered, was not hopelessly fragmented and disunited but interdependent and that the condition of each part depended critically on the health of the whole. The first step toward verifying this proposition was to bring people together to determine whether useful communication, at the simple level of conversational give-and-take, was at all possible.

On opening day the delegates arrived at Princeton, many of them with a measure of skepticism, if not mistrust, over the implied larger goals of the Congress. Coming as they did from vastly different theatrical backgrounds, many were self-conscious and suspicious. When the delegates came face to face and began talking to each other, much of the mistrust disappeared. Still, certain differences, as between a Broadway theatre manager and the artistic director of an experimental theatre group, inevitably remained. Common solutions to everyone's problems were not found.

This report will seek to show that in openly confronting their very real differences the many dissimilar theatre interests that were represented managed to achieve a kind of unity, and the theatre an identity. Almost the most significant decision made by FACT was to continue in being – to hold future conferences and to maintain a continuing organization to conduct the interim business of the delegates. Certain broad areas of action were set out: marketing, government, urban environment, business, foundations, and media. In subject matter they paralleled the panels at the Congress.

FACT decided that theatre required more sophisticated marketing research and development. On the one hand, the Congress recognized the urgent need for attracting a greater audience, if only for economic reasons. On the other, it acknowledged that in the last ten to fifteen years the composition of the audience had altered considerably; the theatre, for the most part passive and accepting amidst this change, had not been sufficiently responsive. FACT recognized that audience expansion depended on the education of younger theatregoers. Secondly, it agreed to undertake a comprehensive study of more productive marketing and promotional strategies. In industry, marketing patterns are in continual flux; one must be prepared for no less in theatre. Community involvement is a close corollary of audience development; the Congress also decided that national seminars would be desirable to train members of a theatre's staff in community relations.

FACT decided that the theatre should become more closely and continuously informed on government in action at every level, Federal, state, and local, in order to exert a timely influence. Although good relations with friendly legislators would be cultivated and maintained, it was clear that any substantial government support, whether in funding or in favorable legislative actions, depended largely on the ability of the theatre to demonstrate its artistic vitality and its significance and importance to the well-being of the greater community extending across state boundaries. FACT also affirmed the desirability of closely examining postal regulations affecting theatre mailings, the building codes, in their application to both profit and non-profit theatres, and tax and regulatory provisions relating to theatre.

FACT recognized the need for theatre to be concerned with the betterment of the urban environment. Theatre has a stake in the quality of the core city in which it is traditionally located. It cannot stand apart from the struggle to maintain the center city as the locus of night life, entertainment, and the dramatic arts, against the counter pull of the suburbs and the lure of television and film.

FACT decided that as the theatre became more fully involved in the community it should commence to seek substantial business support. Since the interests of both business and theatre in the quality of community life run

11

parallel, the theatre can justly solicit funding from business. Business can also assist theatre with marketing skills and fiscal expertise. In order to involve corporations in theatre it was agreed to launch an educational program comparable to the campaigns of the Concerned Citizens for the Arts, which was formed in New York State in 1969 to support the request for higher state arts council appropriations, and to the Partnership for the Arts, which was organized subsequently to do the same job on a national level.

FACT agreed that business giving would be all the more important if, and as, foundation support were cut back. The Congress agreed that ways should be found to use present foundation assistance as leverage on businesses and individuals, while efforts also should be made to make theatre's needs more widely known to private foundations.

FACT was unable to come to any decision on ways to better relations with the press, radio, and television other than by a continued effort to make clear to journalists and editors the prime importance of live theatre in the competition for space, time, and attention. No aspect of the theatre's dealings with the public is more frustrating or provoking than press coverage, including, of course, criticism. This is hardly surprising. As the media panel made obvious, it is peculiarly the area over which the theatre has no control and on which it can at best have but little effect.

Is the theatre understood? Certainly the press has not sufficiently comprehended the vast changes that have taken place in the last ten or so years, and are still taking place, in the structure of theatre — the ways of organizing, supporting, and presenting dramatic events in this country. Yet the press alone is not to blame for misunderstandings and lack of interest. Theatre people themselves have often not appreciated many of the forces at work. The theatre has become stratified in complex ways. This is due to the rapid expansion of the non-profit area under the stimulus of foundation grants, private giving, and government funding through the National Endowment for the Arts and state arts councils; the solid growth of resident professional theatres in city after city; the rise of institutional or continuing theatres in contrast to one-production-at-a-time commercial managers; the gaining idea of company, communal, and cooperative theatre at the expense of "rugged individualism"; the development of a whole area of workshop theatres such as cover New York's spreading Off Off Broadway, where new projects are conceived and experimentation in new theatrical forms goes forward; and the mushrooming of small theatres organized around companies of dedicated actors committed to specific philosophies of theatre.

Steadily climbing production and operating costs have severely reduced the opportunities for new American plays and new dramatic ideas to take root in the commercial theatre of Broadway. This has caused a significant shift. The point of origination of new work has been relocated further across the theatrical scale to simpler stage formations in the non-profit sector. So that new work can more readily be moved and performed throughout the theatrical estabishment, the Congress agreed on the need to set up some mechanism with special funding to facilitate the transfer of plays from non-profit areas to the commercial theatre — on a non-profit basis. A new organization or some existing service organization such as the Theatre Development Fund might be utilized for this purpose, and a search for subsidy begun.

The Congress also agreed that the rules of Actors' Equity which impede the free flow and formation of all kinds of theatre companies should be relaxed. While the ability to transfer and move new work was held to be a desirable goal, no step should be taken to inhibit the flourishing diversity of all kinds of theatre, large and small, conservative and radical, traditional and experimental. The importance of minority and other "alternative" theatre to the health of the whole theatre was strongly endorsed.

FACT brought together many representative groups and leaders. The discussions were vigorous and for the most part productive. Almost every subject of concern was aired. The

13

panels in many instances produced a consensus and blocked out programs of action. The major accomplishment, however, remains one of definition. By bringing together so many disparate forces in theatre, FACT revealed the outlines and principal features of the American theatre of the 1970's. Altered economic and social conditions force new accomodations, encourage new expression. Such changes have been observed and felt by many, but never before fully articulated in a representative assembly of theatre. Through FACT the theatre of the 1970's began to come to terms with itself. The delegates, standing in for many constituencies, developed an awareness and a sense of mutual respect that are expressed in the existence of FACT as an ongoing organization which, it is hoped, will be able to represent the needs, and express the goals, of theatre to a greater public.

II. How the Congress Came About

Significantly, the impetus for FACT came from the commercial theatre. In recent years a number of Broadway producers and managers, meeting informally or officially around the board room table of the League of New York Theatres and Producers, had been searching for a fresh attack on their problems: the cost escalations of putting on plays; the scarcity of material; the deteriorating conditions of Times Square. The mounting severity of these problems, which resisted partial solution, seemed to call for common action on an industrywide scale.

The idea of a theatre conference had occurred to one producer, Alexander H. Cohen, and from time to time he had tried it out on his colleagues without eliciting much response. But when at the end of the 1972-'73 theatre season the topic came up again in a dinner conversation with Gerald Schoenfeld, of the Shubert Organization, the timing was right. In that encounter — the Cohens and the Schoenfelds meeting for dinner at a midtown Manhattan restaurant on a rainy night in late June, 1973 — FACT had its genesis. The subject of their conversation, the state of the theatre in 1973 after four years of unbroken decline on Broadway, is the essential background for the calling of the Congress.

Schoenfeld dated the decline to the 1969-'70 season as measured by the fall off in three of the traditional ways of selling a Broadway show — mail order, theatre parties, and ticket brokerage. All these indices were down. Partially

15

compensating for them was an increase in ticket sales at the box office and in the use of remote ticket booths such as those located in department stores. But until the fall of 1974 no sign of an upturn was to appear.

It was easy to blame deteriorating conditions in the theatre district for keeping people from visiting the theatre as freely as they did in the 1940's and 1950's, and the shabby appearance of Times Square was somehow emblematic of the theatre's declining fortunes. But it went deeper than that. The nature of the trouble showed up statistically in the end-of-season evaluations — in the decline in the number of shows, particularly new plays, and in playing weeks; in the difficulty of finding financing for productions; and in the dark theatres. In 1969-'70, Schoenfeld's decisive year, only 20 new plays opened on Broadway and only half of them lasted longer than two weeks.*

Finding it increasingly difficult to fill the Broadway theatres with new material of their own origination, the Broadway theatre managers turned to revivals and imports and welcomed productions from the non-profit institutional theatres.** Money was hard, and material already developed and proven elsewhere was cheaper to mount on Broadway. At the beginning of the 1972-'73 season the State Attorney General, basing his annual report on submitted financial statements as required by state law, announced that the number of productions filing with his office for the coming

---

* The downward drift continued: in 1970-'71, 16 new plays; in 1971-'72, 23 new plays; in 1972-'73, 19 new plays, and in 1973-'74, 16 new plays. In the five seasons preceding 1969-'70, the average number of new plays opening on Broadway was 32.

** In 1969-'70, *Indians* from the Arena Stage in Washington; in 1970-'71, Paul Sills' *Story Theatre* and *Metamorphoses* from the Mark Taper Forum in Los Angeles; in 1971-'72, *Two Gentlemen of Verona* and *Sticks and Bones* from the New York Shakespeare Festival Public Theatre, *Solitaire/Double Solitaire* from the Long Wharf in New Haven, and *Moonchildren* from the Arena Stage; in 1972-'73, *The Changing Room* from the Long Wharf, *The River Niger* from the Negro Ensemble Company, and *That Championship Season* and *Much Ado About Nothing* from the Shakespeare Festival; in 1973-'74, *A Streetcar Named Desire* from the Vivian Beaumont Theatre and *Candide* from the Chelsea Theatre Center in Brooklyn; in 1974-'75, *Cat on a Hot Tin Roof* from the American Shakespeare Festival in Stratford, Conn.

season was down by a third. Harold Prince, a major Broadway producer with a virtually unbroken string of hits and a ready list of regular backers, complained that this season for the first time he was having trouble raising money for a new musical. Of his two previous shows, both favorably reviewed, one had made only a small profit and one had lost money. He was reduced to advertising for investors in The Wall Street Journal.

As for general conditions in Times Square, the complaints of theatre people rose to a clamor in July, 1972, when for the first time actors joined voices with sorely tried theatre and restaurant owners and producers. To be sure, some progress had been made in cleaning up the area, and the efforts of the Mayor's Office and of the Office of Midtown Planning headed by William G. Bardel were taking effect. The statistics showed a drop in crime in May, 1972, over the previous May. Prostitution had decreased, at least visibly, as the number of patrolmen assigned to the midtown district increased. But much remained to be accomplished, and the danger of the area tipping into all-out pornography was ever present.

The Lindsay Administration's innovative response to the threatened destruction of the theatre district's character, by the inexorable march of large-scale real estate development, was then being put to the test. The formula that allowed developers more tower space if they agreed to incorporate new theatres in their buildings at ground level had created new economic problems, at least in the case of the two largest theatres. Both the Minskoff and the Uris theatres could reach capacity only by booking super-hit musicals or big-name entertainers, and even then they could not break even. The 1,850-seat Uris was opened Nov. 19, 1972, with a musical that cost $800,000 to produce and lasted seven performances. Less than two years after opening, in May, 1974, the Uris building itself was to go into bankruptcy. Had he to do it over again, Jerome Minskoff told a FACT panel, he would not build the Minskoff Theatre.

The real ailments of theatre, as William J. and Hilda

Baumol were to write in The New York Times on June 2, 1974, are not, as commonly thought, labor unions and featherbedding. What they contribute to operating costs is relatively minor. Nor could the blame be put on high ticket prices set by supposedly profiteering producers. The producers were not making exorbitant profits and prices had barely kept pace with inflation. Rather, the Baumols diagnosed theatre's real illness as the "cost disease." While wages rise continuously, the nature of live performance permits very little increase in productivity. Every article and aspect of theatre is handmade, including the unrepeatable dramatic event of the evening's performance. In theatre, peculiarly, there is simply no safety valve to relieve the cost pressure.

It was an almost unnoticed occurrence that was to have greatest impact on the New York theatre of the late 1960's and 1970's. In this period the city was undergoing enormous population shifts. During the 1960's, 900,000 of its white population had fled to the suburbs to escape the familiar urban ills of deteriorating living conditions, housing that had become too expensive, crowded schools, and an increase in crime. The affluent middle-class and upper-middle-class audience that faithfully patronized the Broadway theatre in the 1950's and for most of the 1960's had gone. The pace of this out-migration quickened in the first years of the 1970's. According to a study by the New School for Social Research, based on Census Bureau figures, the flight of white individuals and families, from 1970 to 1973, further depleted the city by more than 400,000. This was accompanied by a rise in black, Spanish-speaking, and Oriental population of more than a quarter of a million. The yearly average emigration of families had jumped from a level of 2,000 a year in the 1960's to 10,500 in the 1970's.

In such shifts and upheavals New York was but the model and most extreme example of changes taking place in other cities. This was the nature of the urban drama being played out all across America. There was no stemming the tide nor softening its deleterious effect on theatre. Most efforts seemed like whistling into the cyclone.

In January, 1971, Broadway instituted a 7:30 curtain in the hope of reviving interest among commuters. But after eight months one major producer, David Merrick, defected. Under pressure from theatre restaurants, ticket brokers, travel agents, garages, and other theatre district interests, the obligatory 7:30 curtain was dropped in January, 1973, so that individual producers could set their own curtain times, usually 7:30 or 8, depending on the nature of the show and its potential audience.

In the early 1970's the Broadway managers were confounded by an extraordinary and especially dismaying new phenomenon. Even supposedly hit shows were not selling out. Even rave reviews were not influencing people to go to the theatre. There was no longer any such thing as a "hard" ticket. Early morning lines at the box office and scalper's prices for hits were relics of the past. An eerie quiet had settled like a pall on the theatre district. The critic Walter Kerr, gazing around him while standing one evening, as he had done a thousand evenings before, at the busiest intersection in the district, suddenly woke to the realization that he was looking out on a ghost town. Writing in The New York Times Magazine on June 3, 1973, Kerr said:

> I *had* felt, for several seasons before, no pressure under the Broadway floor. No ripples, no threat of undulation, no promise that a crack might open and a new creative life peep through. For about 18 out of the 21 years I've been reviewing, it had always been there. Not too powerful, perhaps, but *there,* altering the old order slowly but keeping the street mildly restless just the same. Then, suddenly, it had vanished. You could put your ear to the ground and hear only the subway.

The symptoms of the disease had become painfully obvious. The partial cures administered from time to time — adjusting the curtain hour and exhorting the city to clean up the Times Square district and to cope with the crime and the spreading pornography that seemed to be giving the place the character of an X-district — were no more than palliatives.

19

In May, 1973, just before Cohen and Schoenfeld met, Herman Levin, who had produced *My Fair Lady* at the height of Broadway's post-war prosperity, proposed an industrywide promotion plan to the board of governors of the League of New York Theatres and Producers. Such an effort would be financed by an assessment on all first-class shows playing in New York and on the road amounting to half of one per cent of the box-office gross — a figure calculated to yield $500,000 a year.

Still, something was missing in this approach. As Cohen and Schoenfeld discussed the nature of the problem, there were no piecemeal solutions or cures. Broadway people could not fully comprehend the nature of the forces at work in their own sector of theatre without understanding the nature of the interlocking forces, including the positive factors, at work elsewhere in the theatre. The divisiveness of people living within the same artistic community called for corrective measures. Ultimate solutions lay beyond Broadway's narrow boundaries. Hence the idea of a conference that would permit an industrywide exchange.

That summer Alexander H. Cohen went abroad taking a pile of theatre-related reading with him. Among the books was Margaret Croyden's *Lunatics, Lovers & Poets*, a critical study of the history and aesthetics of the contemporary experimental theatre. Here was a world of theatre unknown to him although in his own backyard, whose influence had spread, and whose ideas indirectly affected him and his colleagues. Returning to New York, he was more than ever persuaded of the importance of a broadly conceived conference. At a board meeting at the outset of the 1973-'74 season, Cohen formally proposed that the League sponsor a national congress that would bring together both the profit and the non-profit theatre. Supported by Schoenfeld, Richard Barr, president of the League, and others on the board of governors, the idea was approved. Cohen, as the originator of the suggestion, was asked to follow through. Among his peers he was uniquely qualified by talent and experience to do so, and he had the backing of a well-staffed office which besides the normal production work handled special projects such as the annual Tony Awards television special. The League voted $20,000 toward the organization and setting up of the conference. That sum was matched by the Independent Booking Office (I.B.O.), which receives fees from producers and theatre managers to arrange national tours of Broadway shows. The Theatre Development Fund (TDF), as a service organization established to encourage the flow of new material of quality into the commercial theatre by audience subsidy and other measures, provided the $8,200 needed to complete Cohen's proposed budget of $48,200.

Later, Cohen solicited further sums to help defray the travel costs or registration fees of delegates — particularly delegates from non-profit groups unable to finance the trips. The Theatre Development Fund, on special application to the National Endowment for the Arts, provided an additional $10,000. The American Theatre Wing gave $15,000 and its president, Isabelle Stevenson, joined the steering committee. Cohen also approached the Exxon Corporation whose interest in theatre was evidenced in its sponsorship of the "Theatre in America" series on public television, a showcase for the outstanding work of regional and repertory companies. Exxon contributed $5,000, to round out the overall conference budget of $78,200.

In the early stages of planning, the steering committee consisted of League members: Cohen, Schoenfeld, Joseph Harris, president of the I.B.O., T. Edward Hambleton, of the New Phoenix Theatre, Warren Caro, of the Shubert Organization, and Richard Barr. When TDF was asked to participate financially, Hugh Southern, its executive director, was brought into the discussions and suggested to Cohen that the committee was not properly constituted to represent the whole of American theatre. At his instigation, new members were added. They were: Dr. William J. Baumol, the Princeton University economist who has conducted a number of surveys for the theatre and co-authored, with William G.

Bowen, the landmark Twentieth Century Fund study, *Performing Arts: The Economic Dilemma,* published in 1966; Stephen Benedict, then of the Rockefeller Brothers Fund, who was president of TDF; Ruth Mayleas, director of theatre programs for the National Endowment for the Arts; Lewis L. Lloyd, then program director for the performing arts, New York State Council on the Arts; Lloyd Richards, director of the National Playwrights Conference of the Eugene O'Neill Memorial Theatre Center and president of the Society of Stage Directors & Choreographers, and Peter Zeisler, president of the Theatre Communications Group.

By December the steering committee was organized and functioning. Meeting with them to plan for the Congress were Richard Hummler, of the Alexander H. Cohen office, and Alfred Stern, a consultant to the Congress. In December and January, Cohen devoted his weekends to a search for a suitable conference site, making a series of motor swings in a 50-75 mile arc around New York City with the help of his staff and Stern. By late January they had settled on Princeton with its conference facilities at the Woodrow Wilson School of Public and International Affairs and living accommodations in the Nassau Inn.

Meanwhile, other members of the steering committee compiled an invitation list of 500 names, and letters of invitation were sent out describing "a working congress to diagnose the problems facing the theatre and, it is hoped, suggest remedies." Topics chosen for discussion were urban deterioration, inflation and economic recession, the need to stimulate youth and minority audiences, coping with rising production and operating costs, and dealing with the unpredictable nature of financial support. Finally, it was hoped that the Congress would be able "to speak with one voice on all matters concerning public subsidy and other forms of aid to the theatre." The steering committee went to work preparing lists of guest speakers and framing questions for the panels to consider.

Replies to the letters of invitation were slow in coming back, partly because of the $350 individual registration fee and partly because those invited needed time to consult with their boards of directors and arrange their schedules for a four-day conference. Eventually, 224 firm registrations were received.

Now, the steering committee, with its expanded membership of 14, began meeting more frequently, first every fortnight, then every ten days, and finally weekly as opening day approached. Initially, Cohen hoped to keep the conference closed to the press in order not to inhibit discussion, but he was dissuaded from doing so after a conversation with Arthur O. Sulzberger, publisher of The New York Times, who expressed the interest of his paper in covering the proceedings. It was agreed therefore to open the conference to the press on a limited basis.

A major theatre meeting similar to this, although without its comprehensive structure, had been called on Broadway during the depression years. But not since then had theatre people come together in such numbers out of a similar sense of urgency. Also in the midst of the Depression the newly formed Federal Theatre under Hallie Flanagan brought the regional and state directors together in Washington for two days of talks with representatives of other theatre groups. This was the formative session of the Federal Theatre, this country's first experiment in a wholly subsidized theatre, backed by WPA funds to give employment to thousands of out-of-work theatre artists. Beginning in the late 1950's the American National Theatre and Academy (ANTA) held a series of national theatre conferences. The first ANTA Assembly was held in the Astor Hotel in New York City in 1959 and the seventh and last in Hollywood in 1966. Still FACT had a legitimate claim to its title of "first."

The FACT delegates, panelists, and special guests came from 17 states, the District of Columbia, and Canada. They represented many different interests in theatre, or allied to the theatre: elected and appointed government officials, theatre company directors and producers, planners and designers, the heads of service organizations of all kinds, foundation executives, educators, critics, writers, reporters, union heads, and attorneys.

Many boarded buses in Shubert Alley on Sunday afternoon, June 2, to make the trip to Princeton in time for the opening reception and banquet at the Nassau Inn and an address by Senator Jacob K. Javits. The Congress operated on a tight schedule of panels, plenary sessions, dinners, and entertainment. The first plenary session was held Monday morning in the auditorium of the Woodrow Wilson School where the desks carried the name cards of all the delegates. Alexander H. Cohen made the introductory remarks and was followed by three scheduled speakers: Richard Barr, W. McNeil Lowry, of the Ford Foundation, and Michael Straight, deputy director of the National Endowment for the Arts, filling in for Nancy Hanks, the director, who was prevented by illness from attending. As soon as the floor was thrown open to questions, the discussion began, and the contrary points of view present made themselves felt.

That afternoon the first two panel discussions, on Legislation in Support of the Professional Theatre and The Media and the Theatre, were held from two to six, with a coffee break in mid-afternoon. The evening entertainment consisted of Sammy Cahn performing the material of his Broadway show, *Words and Music.*

Tuesday morning another plenary session was held, with reports delivered by the chairmen of the first day's panels and an address by Joseph Papp, followed by questions and discussion. After a mid-morning break the next two panels were held, Alternative Theatre, which continued through the afternoon and made for one of the liveliest sessions of the Congress, and Foundations: Criteria and Philosophy. In the afternoon there were two more panels, Technological Developments and Stimulating Creative Resources. Dinner that evening was set aside as free time with no formal events scheduled and later in the evening there were two showings of Louis Malle's film *Lacombe, Lucien* at the Princeton Playhouse.

At the Wednesday morning plenary session there were more reports and a short address by David Merrick followed by a long and frank question period. Three panels commenced work in mid-morning: Legislation Restricting the Professional Theatre, Restoration of the Urban Environment, and Increasing Corporate Support. After a poolside lunch at the Nassau Inn there were reports on these panels. The final FACT panels were held in the afternoon: The Audience for Theatre Today, Innovations in Marketing, and Stimulating Creative Resources (Part II). At the closing banquet that evening the main speaker was Peter Ustinov.

In outline, this, then, was the schedule of the four-day FACT conference. Not everything of importance that transpired at the conference came out of the business sessions alone. Some of the most productive discussions, in the opinion of many of the delegates, occurred informally after hours. Nor did the business meetings necessarily restrict themselves to the assigned topics. The discussion was free-ranging throughout. Certain major themes were sounded early in the conference and reverberated from panel to panel. By virtue of their assigned topics, the panels divided themselves generally into two main categories — those that considered the forces, governmental, quasi-public, and private, acting upon theatre from the outside and the ways they could be redirected to the benefit of the theatre, and those that examined how the theatre could strengthen itself, so to speak, from within. This report will summarize the discussion and decisions of FACT according to these two general groupings and will also attempt to identify the main themes of the conference and what they signify. But first, let us consider the breadth and scope of this conference by excerpting key passages from some of the major addresses.

III. Major Statements

Senator Jacob K. Javits of New York was an altogether fitting choice as opening speaker of the Congress. First in the House, and since 1957 in the Senate, he has represented a substantial theatre constituency longer than has any other elected official. His dedication to theatre is unquestioned, his concern made felt on numerous occasions both in Washington and at home in New York. In 1949 the then Congressman Javits introduced a (largely ignored) bill to establish national theatre. For sixteen years he persisted in proposing government funding for the arts. Such efforts, combined with those of many others, culminated in the passage of the National Arts and Humanities Bill of 1965. He referred to both initiatives in his speech, key passages of which are reprinted below.

Senator Jacob K. Javits

The two things I would like to recommend to your panel are the following:

One. We finally worked out a bill which covered both the arts and the humanities. The arts are now in the hands of two very gifted people, Nancy Hanks and Michael Straight, their panels, and the whole panoply of their activities. The humanities are also in the hands of a very able and gifted man, Dr. [Ronald S.] Berman. There is a great community of interest between the humanities and theatre. Theatre can be used enormously in intellectual pursuits, for teaching, for opening up new horizons. As the Endowment for the Humanities has an equal amount of resources to disburse as the Endowment for the Arts, you should study very carefully how you can tie in with that particular activity. In a very real sense, their activities are much more duplicative of the activities of colleges and universities and learned societies if they remain simply catholic to what the word "humanities" means in its rather narrow sense. But if expanded to include, for example, certain of the activities of the theatre, then they translate into a new dimension. This is a clue, a key, a path which you can point out in your deliberations as you do represent in a very real way the American theatre here.

Two. An expansion of the Endowment of the Arts. That takes time and a lot of effort, but it can be done. That would be an expansion which would allow of joint production between the theatre as it stands and the Endowment, in a way which is advanced from where they are today. The reason for saying that is that when the law was originally developed and thought about by me, the idea I had was that the theatre should go into areas which were not reached; that the commercial theatre, having certain exigencies and demands of its own, should be viable in economic terms — that it had to omit many parts of the country which were considered in the very old days "the road," but which today have to be bypassed simply for commercial reasons.

They shouldn't be bypassed. They should be cultivated and served by this art. The question is how. The Endowment has done very well in that, but if you add the dimension of some form of partnership or relationship or joint venture with the commercial theatre, you may be able to get a much greater outreach than even the Endowment has been capable of up to now. In order to encourage you in thinking about that and trying to develop a methodology in which that can be done, the amounts which we are now providing — though relatively large compared to what we started with — are very small. . . .

Finally, you have a very favorable audience in the Congress.

27

Probably the most extraordinary thing which has happened in government has been the change in the attitude of members of the House and Senate toward theatre and dance and music, etc. . . .

Knowing American politics as I do, that is absolutely fantastic. If you served in the House of Representatives when I did and heard an exhibition of painting which the United States sent abroad through the USIA in the middle 1950's excoriated, laughed at, that the United States should engage in such frippery as sending an art exhibit abroad, and then saw the attitude of sobriety which surrounds our hearings of today when it comes to these issues which I have described, the dignity and strong favor which follows them on the floor of the Senate and of the House, you would grow very proud of the totally new awakening of the intellect and of artistic endeavor in our country.

The Congress got down to business on Monday morning. In introductory remarks to the assembled delegates, Alexander H. Cohen expressed the hopes and expectations of the organizers of FACT. His remarks in their entirety follow.

Alexander H. Cohen

This Congress is the manifestation of an awareness that has existed for several years within the theatre community that we do not function as a unified force. The theatre is one of the last strongholds of rugged individualism in this country. Historically, this has been one of its strengths. Successful theatre cannot be made by committee, and theatre cannot be administered through a bureaucracy. The theatre is a collaborative art, but the collaborators must reflect strongly individual points of view.

It is undeniably a sign of health that in an age of collective thinking and loss of identity, the theatre has remained stubbornly independent. Independence does not preclude

28

interdependence and that is what FACT is all about. This Congress is based on a very simple, very obvious principle. We must recognize and act on that recognition that all of us who work in the American professional theatre have some common problems that admit to common solutions. It is a truism to observe that the professional theatre is in a chronic state of crisis. Broadway, Off Broadway, non-profit professional, experimental — we all work under a sword of Damocles. The sword has different edges for all of us, but it is the same sword, and it is high time that we began to design a common shield.

All of us in this room are in some way expert in the practice of theatre. We have had to be in order to survive. Much of our knowledge is shared, but much of it is particular, special. We all have things to learn from each other.

To facilitate this exchange of information, the steering committee is an eclectic group whose members represent every branch of the professional theatre. The panels have not been tossed together lightly. They represent a distillation of private thought and open deliberation among some very intelligent theatre professionals. We think the results will be invaluable.

The First American Congress of Theatre is a mechanism, a device that can be used or not used. How much of what happens over the course of the next three days will be turned to tangible advantage is now up to you. One thing is certain. We are off to a good start. The attendance of FACT, both qualitatively and quantitatively, is frankly far above our early expectations. Before the Congress' work has really even begun, it is a success because you are here.

I doubt if ever before in the history of our theatre has there been gathered together such an influential group of real activators of the people who make theatre happen. We do not expect to emerge from this convention with bylaws for a national theatre of the United States. This is a beginning. Concrete developments must be slow in coming. We do hope, however, to end this Congress with a firm resolution on the *part of all the participants that it become an annual event. If the Congress achieves what we think it will achieve, that will be a logical outcome. If it doesn't, it won't be worth repeating anyway.*

There is one important truth we should all try to keep in mind for the next few days. As I said, the people in this room represent many different theatre disciplines. The difference in some cases may appear on the surface to be so radical that rapprochement is impossible. I think it will be possible if we remember that we all share a fundamental faith in and commitment to theatre as the most profound of all the arts, the one that speaks most directly and forcefully to us about us. If we keep that in mind, if we accept the fact that we are all on the same side, then FACT will be a success.

Richard Barr came to the presidency of the League of New York Theatres and Producers in 1967 by a circuitous route that led from Broadway to Off Broadway to Off Off Broadway and back to Broadway. His appearance in Princeton before a gathering of theatre people closed a circle of another sort. He was graduated from Princeton University in 1938 and began at once on his career in the theatre by joining Orson Welles' Mercury Theatre and playing a "carry-on" role — in this case, carrying on a pulpit — in *Danton's Death* that fall. In his address, Barr sketched out some events of his own career to throw a personal light on the changing backdrop of American theatre, whose very beginnings, Barr noted, were within reach of the memory of at least some of those present.

Richard Barr

The modern American theatre in which we all here are participating is only about fifty years old. I mark its beginnings with Eugene O'Neill's Beyond the Horizon *at the Morosco Theatre on February 4, 1920. Of course, there was* theatre of interest and importance before 1920, but it was not very original if you except the touring companies, the famous melodramas, or the one unusual piece of work, Uncle Tom's Cabin. . . .

O'Neill, of course, began changing all that. It is important to note two facts about O'Neill's beginning. He started Off Broadway, and he was introduced by a fledgling institution, which later developed into the first major American institution, the Theatre Guild. I'll come back to Off Broadway later, but the point about institutions is of significance because we have had very few institutions indeed in the history of the theatre – that is, permanent or relatively permanent institutions (the Mercury Theatre lasted only two seasons) which showed a continuity of effort. The theatre was, and many believe it still is, a catch-as-can enterprise with many individual entrepreneurs moving in as many directions in one relatively small locale – Broadway.

The concentration in one locale is not of itself noteworthy. Almost all great theatres centered in the capital or major cities of a nation – Athens, Rome, Paris, London. Only Germany developed a system which still exists with the city or state theatre. It should be quickly noted that Germany has produced very few important playwrights. . . .

As the costs on Broadway began to rise, it became necessary to get outside help. First, friends only were propositioned for money. Then inevitably the public. This was a most significant change for the theatre. Beginning as a small personal artistic enterprise, the production of a play moved into a business area. This change marked the start of the problems that are still with us today, and is certainly largely responsible for our being here today. It is impossible, under the present system of seeking public funds, for Broadway to continue presenting plays of serious content. As a matter of fact, it is almost impossible to finance plays of not-so-serious content.

To get back to O'Neill moving to Broadway through the auspices of the Theatre Guild in 1920, exactly forty years later in the same little theatre where O'Neill had begun – the

31

Provincetown Playhouse – and using the same permanent cyc that Bobby [Robert Edmond] Jones had built for The Emperor Jones, *we presented Edward Albee's* The Zoo Story. *It cost $5,000, and I spent $1,000 too much in advance advertising in* The New York Times; *it should only have cost $4,000.*

It is also interesting to note that just as O'Neill moved to Broadway within a year or two after Emperor Jones, *Albee moved to Broadway with* Who's Afraid of Virginia Woolf? *and for the same reason. As long as Broadway remains the theatre capital of the world, playwrights, directors, designers, actors – all who contribute artistically to the theatre – will want to be a part of the Broadway scene. It is still the stamp of approval, and it is still the central money market.*

. . . Almost all the professional theatre in the western world is subsidized in one way or another. Almost all theatre in the western world considers Broadway (there will be no more Off Broadway of any consequence – it has outpriced itself) the capital of the theatre world. Ask any writer, director, actor, or designer what his eventual goal is, and you will get one answer.

I am not being a propagandist for Broadway because I believe all is well, or because I believe we do better work than others, or because I believe we are presenting the most exciting plays or the most daring or the most worthy. I can say what I have said because it is true, and the reason it is true is that there is more money there, and that is all. The fact that a play is presented on Broadway, if successful, simply creates more money for it elsewhere for the contributing artists. It is as simple as that.

No relating of problems we face would be complete without suggesting that the main purpose of this gathering is to break down the dichotomy that exists between the non-profit professional and the Broadway theatre. Until recently, for reasons known to no one, it was very, very difficult – not just expensive – to move to Broadway from Off Broadway as London has done in the West End. It simply

*didn't work. One can cite exceptions, but they were just that
— exceptions. . . .*

The non-profit professional theatre has also another problem. They do not get the first chance at new scripts. I have read over 10,000 new plays. Lloyd Richards of the O'Neill Foundation quoted some figures from his own observation the other day at a meeting of the theatre panel of the New York State Council on the Arts. He matched my observation exactly. He said that of the 800 scripts they read a year for the O'Neill Foundation, maybe 30 were readable, eight were worth thinking about, and one or two were producible in a workshop situation. I agree. From my 10,000, 100 have been readable. Of the 100 or so we presented at the Playwrights Unit, about 10 were producible on a professional basis. That sounds like 10 per cent. It isn't. These were highly concentrated submissions. Generally, the average is one per cent. In my opinion, there are at this time no important American playwrights unproduced professionally. In all of history, Buchner, who died at 22 or 23, was the only playwright not recognized during his lifetime, and I see no reason why that should change.

More new plays were produced in Manhattan last year (I did not say Broadway) than in any other country in the world. The reason for that is that there is an arena there where they can get plays produced. . . . If we can make a continuing exchange between the non-profit professional theatre Off Broadway and, in rare circumstances Off Off Broadway, with Broadway, if we can share and make it easy to transfer in either direction, if we can make it simple for a talented playwright to be heard by subsidizing from either end, if we can begin to think of the American theatre as the American theatre and not just as Broadway or regional, profit or non-profit, if we can do this together in a sensible non-selfish, non-egotistical manner, we have the possibility of equalling Athens.

In his role as deputy director of the National Endowment for the Arts, Michael Straight defined both the extent, and the limits, of Federal support for theatre. The first was remarkable in view of the relatively short period of time in which the government has been supporting the arts. As for limits, he warned that government would not take up the slack as foundation giving dropped. On behalf of the Endowment, he backed the work of FACT and promised continued support.

Michael Straight

The Endowment supports [the professional non-profit theatre companies] in terms of eligibility when they have annual budgets of over $200,000 a year, when they have two years of continuous operation under the same management as professional theatres, when they have performance seasons of at least five months, and Equity contracts or the equivalent in salaries. It makes grants to them of up to $140,000 a year, but no more than one-half of their budgets, and it allocates to them — hopefully in this coming year starting July 1 — a little over $3 million.

Sixty-five of these companies — in itself an extraordinary tribute to the vitality of theatre around the country — applied for support last year. Fifty of them were supported in 22 states and in the District of Columbia. Of those 50, 11 were in New York City. The support varied as a percentage of their budget from 3 per cent in the case of the New York Shakespeare Festival to 6 per cent in the case of A.C.T., 8 per cent for the Guthrie, 10 per cent for the Arena, 21 per cent for the Negro Ensemble Company.

To summarize: first, resident professional companies of any kind are still only struggling to exist and expand in one-half of the states of the United States. Two, they are struggling to expand but more than a third of them overall are in debt. Three, public support by the states' agencies is now established. Four, municipal support — the factor, as Dick [Barr] mentioned, which has been critically important in Germany and important throughout Europe — is almost wholly lacking

34

in this country, due in part to lack of tradition and in part to the great financial insolvency of the cities.

We come here in a common identity of interests. The immediate identic interest in terms of the future is expansion of theatre in the U.S. Expansion is in the interest of commercial theatre when it operates at less than capacity. It is in the interest of companies such as the Arena which is operating at 90 per cent of capacity because it permits the director to raise his standards of production and not to be concerned about the continuous nightmare of . . . capacity . . . It is in the interest of the non-professional which we support indirectly. That non-professional realm is of enormous importance to this group, though it may not be on the agenda as an immediate concern.

It follows that, in terms of planning for us, that which obstructs the expansion of theatre in any form — archaic tax systems, restrictive union regulations, obsolete real estate laws, inequitable taxation of royalties and of author's rights, the insolvency or mediocrity of training institutions — are all matters of common concern which we either take common action in or fail. By the same token, that which expands the theatre is a matter of common concern for all of us, because every group here is committed necessarily to expansion as a way of surviving.

Within this overall framework, however, there are plainly underlying differences of opinion if not of interest within this audience. First, within the community of non-profit theatres, there is an early warning that foundation support is declining as government support increases. Second, within the community of professional theatres, non-profit theatres are expanding at the expense of commercial theatres. . . .

For the individual foundation, the role of starting projects and moving out may be wholly consistent with continuing support, but if foundations as a group assume that when the government accepts some responsibility, to that extent they can abrogate their responsibility, we are then in for a series of jolting shocks. Government support by any absolute standard is very small. It amounts to 35 cents per person. It amounts *to five or six per cent of the budgets overall of the institutions we support. It amounts to one cent in every $35 of the Federal budget, and it is not likely to be rapidly transformed. . . .*

The government will not expand its role to compensate for the lessening role of foundation, of corporations, of individual donors. It will not — and, for the moment, should not — because government lacks the wisdom to become a predominant element in the artistic life of the country. . . .

The feeling nonetheless persists that the non-profit producer is at an advantage, and it is a matter of life and death for the disadvantaged producer, the commercial producer, to share somehow in the advantages which the other has obtained. We operate under the aegis of a view which says we are all theatre, and all theatre is entitled to public support.

To many present, W. McNeil Lowry, last of the three speakers at the first plenary session, personified the beneficence of foundations in the performing arts. He had a long history in this field. During his vice-presidency of its Division of Humanities and the Arts, the Ford Foundation had given grant support to the non-profit professional theatre, amounting to $35.5 million.

W. McNeil Lowry

I feel rather sandwiched in between the very trenchant economic and other analyses of Mr. Baumol and Mr. Cohen and Mr. Barr and Mr. Straight — who just told me something I didn't know about foundations, on the one hand, and something I am concerned about, on the other. He told me that the private foundation did a project and then quit. With some of the theatres, we are in grants that are in their seventeenth year, and I don't know when they can quit.

In response to the very great concern expressed by the New York State Council, if the large national foundations do less next year or the next year or the year after that than they have done in theatre, it will not be because of government support — Federal, state, or municipal — because government support is a minor factor, though a most welcome one, in the whole picture. I could not agree more with Mr. Straight's demand, his plea that foundations persist in this effort. . . .

[The Ford Foundation] did not move into theatre to create or to strengthen all the institutions of theatre . . . It moved because [hundreds of theatre] artists rightly or wrongly said that the conditions of the commercial theatre were such that . . . it was very hard for a serious actor . . . to work under conditions that made them feel they had a craft, to work to their capacities, and it was very hard to play very many roles that they regarded as important to them and through which they wanted to express themselves. . . .

Counting all its work with playwrights, actors, directors, designers, Off Broadway and Off Off Broadway, occasionally establishing a new theatre company as the Negro Ensemble, giving support to the non-profit resident theatres . . . $35.5 million or 52.4 per cent [of arts money] comes from the Ford Foundation. The other 47.6 per cent has come equally at about $15 million from the National Endowment for the Arts and the Rockefeller Foundation . . . and 4 per cent or $2.7 million from the Mellons and their antecedents. . . .

Will the Ford Foundation continue to make a priority of theatre? Yes, and of the other creative and performing arts. There is a great deal of talk, all of it accurate, about what is happening to the portfolios of national foundations, and there may be a lull in the actual size of the funds available for the theatre or any of the other arts, but there will be no diminution of the Ford Foundation in the arts. . . .

"Is the commercial theatre on Broadway to be subsidized?" was a subject that was certainly telegraphed here this morning . . . . I have no objection to this. I do know that it would not be something that the national foundations would immediately leap to unless they had what some people tell me my new foundation is going to have . . . They said it was going to have masses of millions . . . . There is a dichotomy *between commerce and art in my mind. The first press release put out by the Ford Foundation, when it got permission for a national program in the arts and we had the magnificent sum then of $1.6 million for the entire creative and performing arts all over the country . . . said that theatre in this country was a cultural resource equal to music and the visual arts and ought to be regarded as such. That is the thesis on which all of us are working.*

Of the FACT delegates and speakers, Joseph Papp, principal speaker at the plenary session Tuesday morning, represented the greatest variety of activity. The range of productions in recent years extended from workshops to first-class Broadway presentations, accompanied by all the panoply of the commercial arena. His multiple constituencies include non-paying audiences for Shakespeare in Central Park and season subscribers at Lincoln Center. The Congress organizers looked to him to bridge the gulf between the worlds of theatre. The delegates wanted to hear how, amidst such diversity, artistic integrity could be maintained. It was consistent and in keeping with Papp's style that he should open not defensively but by challenging the idea of the Congress itself.

Joseph Papp

I was very concerned about coming here. In fact, I didn't want to. The reason may have something to do with the whole nature of conferences, particularly on so vast a subject. Conferences can be very boring mainly because a lot of people talk to themselves. It is also extremely difficult to come away from a conference with one idea that is viable. What we generally get is a rehash of a lot of things that most of us know in one form or another, but we develop a kind of confrontation with various groups, particularly under this circumstance where we are thinking of an ecumenical kind of situation — and I am not just talking about the commercial theatre versus the non-commercial, because within the non-commercial there are 70 to 80 splinters, elements, all having their own identity, all having their own function, all having their own artistic views, all having their own concerns. . . .

As to why this conference was held, I . . . assume the worst. One, the commercial theatre operators were very interested in obtaining government support, because the industry is ailing, and they would like to exploit the energy or the purity of the non-profit sectors and some way, for their purposes, to say, "Let's all get together, boys, so that we are all speaking with one voice." The worst thing in the theatre is one voice. It is the multiplicity of voices that makes us all so interesting. . . .

My feelings today are that the crisis in the theatre is very much related to the crisis in the United States and the crisis in the world. The world is in a very heavy crisis . . . The cities are in the state of massive change, not necessarily for the better, but we must recognize the change if we are going to at least live with some kind of consciousness of what is going on.

I don't see any major changes in the theatre, except through individual expertise, individual conviction, individual thrusts at various walls in trying to break them down, unless it is connected totally with what is changing and happening in this country. The devastation throughout the world today is remarkable, and one always feels in the theatre that unless we can some way come close to that in our expressiveness, why put it on the stage. One begins to feel a sense of obligation, as supposedly purveyors of ideas about life, people, society, and society all around us is going through the violent throes. . . .

Let me give you an example of a two-headed beast — Lincoln Center, the Beaumont . . . This particular edifice was serving a particular class of people and necessarily so because this class was the people who paid the money. They were people who went to the theatre or the opera or ballet or the symphony. So coming into a situation like that, I wondered if it were possible to alter it in some way. What does one do in a place like that? Twenty-five thousand subscribers existed, mostly people interested in middle European plays, something to reinforce certain traditional feelings, make one feel secure that there are some values that do stand up, that not everything is unmoored, that we are not flying through space now. What does one do with those people?

First of all, we don't want to lose them because the box office depends on people like that. On the other hand, we don't want to suck. So we try to accommodate certain areas of that public within your own integrity. If you are going to do a classic, you hope it is a very fine classic, and you hope that the performers are performers of distinction. On the other hand, you also cannot accept the status quo of those walls, because they are crushing. They want to absorb you and make you like them so that you are not noticed. Consequently, twice a day you have to break the walls down. . . .

The way I am going to survive at Lincoln Center is to recognize certain truths — that it is a showcase basically. It is not the place I work. Most of the work happens downtown [at the Public Theatre] where work is developed with about five or ten workshops going at the same time where there is a process and where failure is not so damaging. It is amazing how we manage to survive after repeated onslaughts by the press. One would think that after two or three plays get hit real bad you would go under. The thing that keeps this theatre and others like it alive is the continuity of artistic purpose or social purpose or combination of both, that there is a consistency of work that has a single drive. It is not a potpourri of work; it is not a supermarket kind of concoction of this play, that play, this play, that play, but a kind of driving idea, and that permanence keeps it together.

As far as the commercial theatre is concerned, it would be foolish to try to connect the commercial theatre with the Off Broadway and the Off Off Broadway theatres. They have almost nothing in common. There are creative producers in the history of the commercial theatre who have had a consistent viewpoint — I keep thinking of Kermit Bloomgarden . . . and others, some of them here, who have tried to do a particular kind of play on Broadway and have lost a lot of money doing so. But still, even with this personal kind of continuity in their particular viewpoint, the pressures and the enormous burden of success make it virtually impossible to really be artistically selective in the way we would like to be in the non-commercial theatre. There is no great thing about being in the non-commercial theatre. We can turn out as great trash if not greater than the commercial theatre, given half a chance! Not only that, but the work sometimes can be very poor. So it is not a question of artistic competition. This is superior. There is no question that if you can get together certain highly creative elements in the proper kind of circumstances, you will produce good work anywhere, whether it be in a Broadway house or an Off Broadway house or some place out west of the Hudson River. . . .

There must be a value here that must emerge out of this conference. As for support for the commercial theatre, all good plays should find some way of getting on the boards. TDF was the first major organization to deal with this problem. The question of profit or non-profit is not a factor either in creative talent nor should it be in terms of plays. We have no playwrights speaking from this forum, which has struck me as rather strange. Since the playwright is one of the key forces in this theatre, there perhaps should be more representation by a major address on the subject. *

My feelings about the commercial theatre in terms of support is that some device should be worked out where serious plays do get some kind of support from a revolving fund, and this money is to be repaid if the play should make it — which is very doubtful, because most serious plays for the most part don't make it in the Broadway sector, because the Broadway sector has changed so drastically.

How do we get into the cities is the main question. Since

* Ed. Note: A number of playwrights were invited to the Congress; few accepted.

41

we are getting support from the government, somehow to deal with the problem we must get out to the great majorities of people in some form, shape, or manner. This is being done on some very small scale today ... One thing nobody knows is how to get people into the theatre .... Basically it must start in the schools. We are talking here about short-range projects, but in terms of the long-range if we are really interested in the arts and the theatre for the future of the children, it must become part of the regular curriculum of the primary schools.

David Merrick appeared before the Congress on the morning of its third, and last, day, an already legendary figure in the commercial theatre, with an uncounted list of hits to his credit, and an undisguised impatience with conferences that indulged, as he said, in hot air, jealousies, and controversy, and which failed to come to the point — how to get more money for the theatre. In his formal remarks Mr. Merrick was brief and teasingly dismissive of the Congress, but in the question period he was candid and helpful, speaking as he did from long and unparalleled experience.

David Merrick

First of all, the non-profit theatre should be taken care of. Yes, the commercial theatre is getting to the point where theatre owners are all losing money; theatres are dark, and they will either turn them into office buildings or parking lots or something. It is absolutely necessary to go in that direction. In case you don't know — it is rather new — the Arts Council in Great Britain, the subsidized theatre in Great Britain, has been the life of the theatre in England. Virtually all the good stuff comes out of the Royal Shakespeare, the National, the Royal Court, the various provincial subsidized theatres. Whether it has already started or not, at least it is very imminent that the Arts Council is now going to supply half the financing for commercial producers in the West End.* That is on a profit-making basis. If we can dig enough money out of it to help the so-called commercial theatre, to augment it, I am all for that too because that is falling apart. . . .

I had an experience some years back. The League of New York Theatres, when I was a member, picked me to go down to Washington to represent the theatre in getting the excise tax taken off our tickets . . . I spoke for five minutes, then ten minutes, for fifteen minutes, and nobody stopped me. Then they started asking questions. They were deeply interested, and the questions were just out of ignorance. They kept me an hour and a half. A.T.&T. got five minutes. What struck me is that they didn't know much about our business and what the theatre meant to the whole of the country. Altogether, to them, culture had something to do with bacteria!

When I left there, I thought that if we ever had a group representing all of us go down there, we could make considerable headway in terms of help from the government. How? They give a depletion allowance to the oil people to encourage them to speculate for a natural resource that we have. We already have a special tax setup in the commercial theatre in the limited partnerships. We are able in our limited partnerships to deduct the entire loss that takes place on a play on the basis of its being a wasting asset. That is unusual. Other companies that are formed and are losers can't do that. Why shouldn't the theatre get a depletion allowance to make it more attractive for backers to come in and put money into shows? Could we get it? I think we could if we went down to Washington as a group. That includes the unions, the Dramatists Guild, the Choreographer's guild. If everybody went and made an intelligent plea in that direction, we would make headway. It wouldn't happen in the next few months; it would take time, and we would get it.

* Ed. Note: See Chapter V

What they were particularly interested in was my conten-
tion that the theatre was not simply the few theatres
scattered around the country mostly in New York, but rather
its total impact on the nation in general. My argument was
that the theatre was the spawning ground for 75 per cent of
the talent that winds up on television, working in films,
directors, writers, scenic designers, costume designers, every
aspect of it, were trained originally in the theatre – Off
Broadway, on Broadway, some place . . . That hasn't been
brought home to politicians.

At the final banquet the featured speaker was Peter
Ustinov. Actor, playwright, director, novelist, star of radio,
television, records, and films, he was, in Alexander H.
Cohen's phrase, a true Renaissance man whose expertise even
encompassed meetings similar to the FACT Congress. He
brought the deliberations to a close on a warm note of humor
and good will.

Peter Ustinov

I have been to these sorts of things before, and I must say
that you are so far ahead of the game because what is
interesting here is not the solutions you reach but the
arguments you use to reach them. It is like a French law case.
I am not in the least interested in law cases in England,
because people are too keen to know the results. The French
don't give a damn about the result but want to know the
arguments which led up to it. They don't care whether she
murdered her husband or not; they want to know why! Out
of that comes something very rich and very lively.

Even today at lunch when I heard some people complaining
that not enough time had been allocated to this, that, or the
other, the arguments were going on with redoubled intensity
while we were eating our sausages and drinking our Cokes.
That is very important because it creates contacts which

usually on these occasions are much too formal and much too removed. It is for the privilege of meeting a lot of people. One cannot foretell the value of this meeting. It is much more valuable than people think, even when they are paying it compliments, because it is not in the motions which are passed. It is in the contacts which are made and which will last for many years.

IV. Is the Theatre One or Many?

(THE DEBATES OF THE PANEL ON ALTERNATIVE THEATRE)

The first statement spoken at the Congress to provoke serious challenge — a reference to Broadway as being the ultimate goal of all theatre artists — came midway in the second address at the first plenary session when Richard Barr said, "As long as Broadway remains the theatre capital of the world, playwrights, directors, designers, actors — all who contribute artistically to the theatre — will want to be part of the Broadway scene." Mr. Barr was emphasizing the rewards of money and recognition still available uniquely on Broadway. Nevertheless, his words were as a red flag to many present and, as soon as the floor was thrown open to questions, brought swift rebuttal from Andre Gregory.

"If we are really to do business here," said Gregory, "we must face reality and not deal with fantasies . . . That may have been true four or five years ago. At that time it was even my goal. It isn't true today. Speaking for myself and many other directors, designers, and actors, their goal is not Broadway."

This exchange early in the Congress, which as Gregory suggested could not have occurred just a few years before, illustrated the extent to which new forces in the theatre had diverged from the old. For reasons that might be philosophical, moral, economic, or simply geographic, many delegates had turned away from Broadway theatre. Theatre was no longer shaped in the form of a pyramid with Broadway as its apex. The disagreement that was only touched on in the

46

Barr-Gregory difference, and was the key to many other divisions, was to erupt into heated argument in the panel on Alternative Theatre, at moments the most painful but ultimately perhaps the most satisfying event of the Congress.

We must examine the often extreme and angry statements made at that panel to understand how the Congress dealt with its diversity — the theatre as many — before it could begin to achieve an underlying unity — the theatre as one.

As artistic director of the Manhattan Project, Andre Gregory spoke for the experimental wing and, less directly, for the militants of that wing represented by Richard Schechner, Judith Malina, and Julian Beck; for the black theatre, which Gilbert Moses separated out as "the alternative to the alternative theatre"; for theatre groups whose artistic drive related to the needs of specific audiences, such as those of Hazel Bryant and Luis Valdez; and finally for the resident professional, or regional, theatre as represented by Gordon Davidson of the Mark Taper Forum in Los Angeles, who said:

> One phrase that I have heard around these halls that should be struck from the vocabulary is "try-out." I do not try out plays. I do plays. I make theatre. If a play or a production happens to visit another town and that town happens to be New York City, fine. I am not putting down New York and I know that it is a kind of market-place. But conceptually in terms of the tone and quality of this Congress, theatre is being made throughout the U.S. and it has as much meaning and importance and reverberation for the community in which it is being made as it does in New York City. It is very important that people come to grips with that.

Five years before, "How can I get to New York and make it?" was the question heard most often by Vera Mowry Roberts, chairman of the Theatre & Cinema Department of Hunter College, while travelling, as she has done, 85,000 miles cross country. In the last two years the question had become, "I am going to make theatre where I am."

Richard Barr had spoken out of a wide and catholic theatre experience, which included Off Broadway as well as Broadway production and his presidency since 1967 of the League of New York Theatres and Producers. He received support from a somewhat surprising quarter. Joseph Papp – the producer of the New York Shakespeare Festival, who in the previous two seasons had moved four productions to Broadway and is now, in addition to his multiple downtown activities, the producer for the Vivian Beaumont Theatre in Lincoln Center – found that Broadway offered special possibilities in the broader sort of audience available, in the greater attention and recognition a good play received, and in the amounts of money paid out to the participating artists.

"If I open a play at Lincoln Center, which is like the Broadway area," Papp said, "that playwright gets $15,000 to $20,000 for six weeks. This means that he can sit down for a year and write a play and not feel that he is just wasting his time and being gobbled up by the other medium."

Yet it was Papp, also, who defended the diversity of the Congress as entirely healthy and right, and vital to preserve. For him it was no disadvantage to separate the broad categories of commercial and non-profit, New York and regional, traditional and experimental. Indeed, it was essential to maintain the distinctions between the individual groups and theatres and not let them become fuzzy or fused.

"You each have your own life, and a very special one and a very interesting one," Papp told a plenary session. "Off Broadway is different from Off Off Broadway and certainly different from the commercial theatre. They should not be pushed into the same bag."

He did not believe in an easy interchange between the non-profit theatre and the commercial theatre, as was discussed in the panel on Stimulating Creative Resources.

"How can the mobility of material be facilitated between the non-profit and the commercial theatre? I don't think that will ever work ... The idea that the so-called commercial theatre is going to have a direct relationship to the non-commercial theatre in terms of scripts sounds to me like a pipe dream."

From the floor the critic Marilyn Stasio asked, "Why did

you choose to stress the differences between the various people here and not the areas of common bond and interest?"

Papp drew a distinction between the public position a theatre took and its special artistic character.

> I said that the only common bond of interest is that we are concerned about theatre. The commercial people are concerned because the industry is really in bad shape. It is a crisis situation, and if I were in the government I would say let's do some immediate kind of work for that industry. The city would be involved in it immediately because it is a major economic force in New York City just on pure economics alone. I said that we are together in terms of our desire on a political basis to try to receive money for the arts. The key thing is to get money for the arts, to get as much money as possible. Money is the thing. In that sense we are all the same. The only differences are good differences. I like those differences. They are very healthy.

The panel on Alternative Theatre was arranged to give voice to these differences and allow the various groups that comprised the non-profit sector to define their aims and explain their work to those who knew them only by name and had not before been exposed to the work. For some delegates, such as Joan Sandler, executive director of the Black Theatre Alliance in New York, the panel would also help balance the scales weighted in favor of Broadway.

> I was concerned with what the tone of the conference seemed to be — that you are not doing it right and you are not doing it in a meaningful way unless you go to Broadway, and I utterly disagree with that. That tendency has a destructive element in it. Although there may be some meaningful exceptions to that, the tone of the whole conference seemed to be taken up with the larger capital kind of productions in the theatre, and it has done an unfortunate disservice to many of us attending this conference.

With the exception of the Living Theatre, whose beginnings were in the early days of Off Broadway in the late 1940's, most of the "alternative" theatres sprang up in the revolutionary 1960's, some in response to the civil rights struggle, others motivated or stimulated by the Vietnam War protest, the youth rebellion, and participatory democracy. Largely unnoticed by the conventional theatre, but growing healthily from increasing foundation and government support, the movement expanded invisibly in strength and numbers until it could no longer be considered merely a minority theatre or a freakish aberration. Responding to the political realities of the time, sensitive to the shift in moral values, it cast aside the old formulas. It developed new sets of aesthetics that dictated new modes of training and behavior for performers and altered the old accepted relationships between playwright and director, between actor and audience. If not overtly, it was implicitly a political theatre, and its politics was thrust forcibly on the audience for the Alternative Theatre panel.

The first business of the panel — the arrest and detention of the members of two admired theatre groups in Brazil, Oteatro Oficiana and Grupo Pao E Circo, and of their directors, Jose Celso Correa Martinez and Irma and Luis Do Ze — called for unanimity. This fundamental issue of free expression found the panel session on Alternative Theatre responding with a show of international theatre solidarity. The panel agreed to take the issue before the whole Congress and to send a letter protesting the arrests to the President of Brazil. The protest was organized by the International Theatre Institute of the United States headed by Rosamond Gilder and Martha Coigney. Seven pages of signatures were collected — virtually everyone present signed. The key paragraph read:

"We are dismayed that the valuable contribution to your culture of artists such as these is being prevented and must tell you that the news of these people's arrest and detention casts a shadow upon this Congress where we have gathered to support the freedom and diversity of cultural institutions."

Thus the Congress affirmed for others, as for itself, the right of the free stage to speak out without restriction, especially within a dissenting and disapproving society, and the need of the stage to be defended against the enmity of a ruling or dominant order whenever the stage practices that most vital of its functions — to be disturbing, provocative, and unorthodox. Whether due to the letter or to other factors, within several weeks of the dispatch of the letter the theatre groups detained in Brazil were released.

From this initial point of agreement, the panel moved directly into controversy, with the first speakers calling into question the motivations of the commercial theatre interests in organizing FACT. Gilbert Moses led off:

> What concerns us is the fact that this conference is organized by businessmen to become a national lobby for government subsidy for commercial theatre. There is no reason to stop that machinery from taking place. We can, however, discuss the importance of the kind of theatre we do, and try to make this group as a whole understand that there needs to be an investigation of the values system and the structure.

Moses was a founder of the Free Southern Theatre which was started in 1963 in Jackson, Mississippi, to bring theatre into deprived areas of the South. It began on an integrated basis to see "if theatre can be a form for an idea" and to mirror the kind of society it wanted to see achieved. But in time the idea of bringing culture into these communities changed emphasis to the development of the indigenous culture and the fashioning of plays that came out of local situations. Moses continued:

> If the commercial theatre is going to be subsidized it means that the same structure will exist. It means that those who are losing money will be subsidized by government and they will continue to do the same things. We have to investigate whether that is important to us or not. The proliferation of theatre is the most important thing.

Following Moses, Richard Schechner challenged the conventional theatre, carrying the discussion into controversy. "We are talking about power . . . There is a possibility of a shift in the power and that is why these businessmen are interested. They are losing power. The commercial theatre is the sickest part commercially of an already desperate capitalist situation."

Later in the panel one of those "businessmen," Bernard B. Jacobs, was to answer these and subsequent accusations. Schechner, whose special talent was to be "very quick with words in tense situations," as he said himself, had helped start the Free Southern Theatre. He had been editor of the Tulane Drama Review, later The Drama Review, and is now a professor of drama at New York University as well as co-director of The Performance Group whose artistic specialty is the study of audience-performer relationships.

Schechner attacked the very people who had organized the Congress. "Do we want to lend our support to subsidizing a system which many of us oppose? . . . Why torpedo a ship for ten years, and then when it is going down help to rescue it?"

Perhaps, he suggested, power had shifted so decidedly that his group now held the upper hand. "What price shall we exact?" he asked. "We are in a negotiating situation. Maybe for the first time we are in a powerful situation, and why be generous? When were they generous to us in a similar situation?"

Julian Beck questioned the moral right of a theatre he said catered to the privileged to accept public money. The panelists were becoming entrenched behind a wall of anti-Broadway rhetoric; in the audience there was a growing uneasiness. Alexander H. Cohen replied indignantly to their charges, demanding to know when subsidy for him had been asked of them:

> We are here first of all because we are trying to find common problems and, if there are common problems, find common solutions. I happen to be an independent producer. I don't give a damn about subsidy, and if you gave it to me I wouldn't take it. I want to do what I want to do when I want to do it and how I want to do it, and I am not interested in hearing anybody's opinion about what I do after I've done it.

52

Cohen later explained to the Congress that he referred here to his personal inclinations but stood with his colleagues in welcoming indirect forms of subsidy such as tax abatement, possible depletion allowances for investors, and the repeal of restrictive legislation for the commercial theatre.

The source of the money — the very nature of money — angered Judith Malina.

> What was said here as an opening statement is that the money that represents the source of this funding is already ripped-off money. When Barry [Opper] says importantly that some of us shouldn't be here and when the whole question is brought up as to whether we want to engage at all in a Congress which deals with the whole question of this particular money, which we consider blood money and dirty money, and how do we want to deal with it.

At this point the discussion broke into angry argument between Judith Malina and Ralph Alswang, the designer, who demanded from the floor that she explain the responsibility of the Living Theatre in accepting German money during its subsidized European tours. This, too, was blood money, she agreed; the acceptance of virtually any support posed impossible moral dilemmas for groups such as her own.

In a doubtlessly temporary lull in its stormy history, the Living Theatre at this time was situated in Brooklyn. The forced departure from their stage home on Sixth Avenue and Fourteenth Street, where a remarkable and exciting chapter in Off Broadway artistic history had been written, had come ten years before. There followed the itinerancy of the European period, the sensational return to the United States in 1968 with three ambitious new productions, the residency in Brazil, and the expulsion of the group on trumped-up charges. Now Julian Beck and Judith Malina and a company of 25 were living in two adjoining houses in Brooklyn, supporting themselves through lecture tours, workshops in universities, and royalties from their books and records while planning their next move. They envisioned a type of street theatre dealing with local issues and necessitating new dramatic forms that might take another year to develop.

53

They expected to locate next in Pittsburgh.

Judith Malina went on:

> If we want to rip some of this foundation money back
> how dirty do we have to get our hands? How much do we
> have to kowtow to anyone and be told what to do? None
> of us want to be told what to do with our money when we
> have it. This in some way tears everyone of us here apart,
> because we are also questioning whether we should talk to
> big business about the money that they have earned in a
> way that we think is corrupt. We are all here to wrestle with
> the angels of this problem, to wrestle with the angels of our
> good conscience and our dirty hands, and to decide
> whether it is right in order to present theatre for people in
> the streets, in the barrios, in all ethnic minorities, for the
> kind of thrust we are trying to make — is this a value to the
> businessman? If it is, we must question it profoundly.

Not everyone on the panel shared the militancy of the
Becks and Richard Schechner. It remained for Miguel Pinero
to dispel the moral niceties of the blood money discussion.
The needs of his group overrode having any such scruples as
to the source of support. Pinero is the playwright for The
Family and the author of *Short Eyes,* the prison drama
produced by Joseph Papp in the spring of 1974 at the Vivian
Beaumont Theatre. Pinero thought of his theatre as a means
of survival for the street kids and ex-inmates who made up
The Family and a second group, The Young Family.

> They are kids from the street gangs, juvenile detention
> centers, kids with no parents, out of the drug scene, out of
> the gang scenes. I took off their colors and they are not
> gang fighting, but I have no bread for these kids. When
> some kid says to me, "Mike, I'm hungry," he doesn't stop
> to think where the dollar I'm giving him came from. So I
> think all that about where the money comes from is all jive,
> and we shouldn't even be dealing with that. It is our own
> guilt that makes us villains or heroes or whatever.

Like Pinero, Luis Valdez and Hazel Bryant, who were next
to speak, were involved in an idea of theatre in which
dramatic aesthetics were stimulated and heightened by their

social goals. Unlike their fellow panelists, they were more
activist than theoretician. Valdez, the founder of El Teatro
Campesino, a farm workers theatre organized in 1965 at the
beginning of the California grape strike, shifted the discussion
from money to a Marxian concept of work.

> When political people, if they can be described as that,
> complain and protest, it is because there are people who are
> handling the very symbol of work — money — without ever
> having done any work. Work, as we see it in our group, is
> something that unifies, something that humanifies. It is
> through work that we find our humanity with each other.
> When we talk about revolution, or something like that,
> we are really talking about taking money away from those
> people who never work and giving it to the people who
> rightfully deserve it. It is through our work that we deserve
> the money that we get.

The theatre of Valdez, formed on the picket lines to ward
off what was seen as police and grower harassment,
performed also at union meetings. "Our only aesthetic was
the aesthetic of the factual politics at that time," Valdez said.
In 1967, the theatre broke away from the United Farm
Workers to become independent and is now reorganized into
El Centro Campesino Cultural. Developing facilities on 40
acres at San Juan Baptista, it seeks to encourage all aspects of
the cultural life of the workers. Valdez, now and later in the
panel, was warmly received by the audience for his tempered
remarks.

The greatest applause at the morning session of the
Alternative Theatre panel was reserved for Hazel Bryant's
moving statement about the work of her Afro-American
Total Theatre on the streets of New York. She said:

> What we are really talking about is the haves and the have
> nots. What we have brought to this conference is people
> who have money and people who do not and people who
> do not have the slightest idea how to get the kind of money
> you are talking about, and people who glory in finding
> ways to do what they want to do without money.
> The theatres of myself and my colleagues are involved in
> not just doing theatre but trying to rebuild communities

and lost souls and disappointed people — not just people who are hungry, but people who have heard a lot of promises and they are tired of it, because they don't believe in anything anymore. . . .

So when we put on a production, it isn't just about putting on a glorious play with lots of feathers and fans and lights and all of that. It is about making the people in those seats that you worked damn hard to get in there feel when they go out that they are somebody.

. . . I no longer have the problem of conscience about where the money is and how I am going to get it, because the people I am bringing into my theatre and these other people are bringing into their theatres need it to rebuild their bodies and their souls.

Far from counting herself among those who felt they did not belong at the Congress or should leave the Congress, Hazel Bryant would *use* the Congress.

In a society where money is so desperately important, it becomes very difficult for people who do not have money to have a strong voice. That is one of the ways that you who have money can help us. . . .

So what we are talking about here is all of us looking each other in the eye as men and women at this conference — not who is most important and who isn't, because we already know that. That is a foregone conclusion. So now it is about how do we make all of us important and by so doing, we make people important.

She finished to applause, and the morning session was almost over. There was time for only a few more statements, and Bernard Jacobs, of the Shubert Organization, speaking for a theatre that had been under heated attack, made his reply.

There is a misconception among all of you in terms of creating the impression that there is a we-they. As I see it, there is no future for the profit theatre as we know it. If there is going to be a theatre that survives in this country, it has to be a theatre which is going to produce all the things that all of us want to produce. All the diverse points of view that we have should be represented. It is very important that all of us remain together. Every time one of you gets excited and threatens to walk out as you did yesterday and again today, you do all of us a great disservice, because there is a common approach to theatre that we all have. Those of us who are on our side of the table, if you want to call it that, really are on your side of the table. We are interested in doing everything that we can to help your kind of theatre, because theatre will not otherwise survive in this country. The real issue is do you want theatre to survive, do you want live performances to survive, or do you want the whole thing to die. It isn't a matter of the commercial theatre dying. Each time any part of the theatre, commercial or otherwise, dies, a part of each dies with it.

This statement by Bernard Jacobs contained one of the most quoted remarks of the Congress — "There is no future for the profit theatre *as we know it*." The qualifying phrase (italics added) somehow got lost in the quotation, and Jacobs, powerfully identified with Broadway as one of the Shubert managing directors, temporarily became identified also with an admission that for Broadway the show was over. His remarks were intended not to lower the curtain on Broadway but to express conciliation and concession after a bitterly argumentative morning. It was a way of saying the old image of Broadway had really changed; widely separated as the extremes of theatre had been in the past, profit-making from non-profit, they were much closer both in spirit and in economics today. It was on this note of accomodation that the panel broke for lunch.

The afternoon session was devoted very largely to lengthy statements by each of the panelists about the history, methods, work, and goals of his theatre group. Still, one final political argument was to erupt before they were done. Toward the end of the afternoon, Bernard Jacobs, who felt a kind of accomodation had been reached at the end of the morning, detected once again "the same contemptuous sound to your voice about Broadway."

Neither Schechner nor the Becks were in any way willing to back down from their earlier denunciations of Broadway and their essentially anti-capitalist rejection of the commercial theatre structure. To Schechner, pleas for everyone to get together because they were really in the same boat had the ring of an unacceptable liberalism, and although he could respect what Jacobs did in the theatre he could neither agree with it nor give up trying to see it changed.

For his part, Jacobs could not understand the desire of some alternative theatre members to see Broadway destroyed when Broadway theatres were perfectly willing to welcome their productions. "On your terms," Schechner interjected. When Jacobs protested that they were not *his* terms so much as those of the controlling unions, Julian Beck, with a hint of the belligerence that was to burst forth dramatically in another moment, suggested that those unions, if not the creatures of Broadway, were created in response to the Broadway system.

Judith Malina joined in Schechner's denial of the possibility of liberal accomodation to a system that ultimately, she said, was responsible for war, starvation, suffering, and the exploitation of a bottom class. After she described Broadway as "a strong cultural footstool" for this destructive system, the voice of her husband, Julian Beck, rose angrily above a confused chorus of protests from the floor. Shouting his key words and phrases for dramatic effect, he celebrated the death and destruction of a "dying" Broadway:

> The Broadway theatre makes it possible for the oppressive people to get THEIR CASE and in that way it is part and parcel of the mechanism of OPPRESSION. It is not liberated. It enforces an entire system of thought, of stars, of culture which come out of areas that are alienated to our current needs. THEREFORE, IT MUST PERISH. The alternative theatre is a theatre which has always been opposed to the Broadway theatre. We want to destroy it. It is now being destroyed. It is in fact dying, and THAT IS GOOD.

To more than one member of the audience, Beck's rhetoric was offensive, and to John E. Booth, of the Twentieth Century Fund, who was the first president of the Theatre Development Fund, it sounded like "a dictatorship at work when I, as a member of the audience, am told I no longer have a choice."

Yes, Judith Malina said, he could have his choice of any kind of theatre, but, "What you don't have the choice and what I don't give you the right to do is to kill the children of Indo-China, to support the structure that kills the children."

Once again, amid a volley of objections, Julian Beck delivered another ringing denunciation of the government, the system, and the conventional theatre structure supported by the system "to enforce oppressive cultural forms on masses of people."

After this final outburst, as the end of the afternoon approached, Luis Valdez, in a quiet voice, suggested the one sort of accommodation that was left to those who all day had held so heatedly and so irreconcilably to their positions.

> We see the greatness of the Living Theatre precisely in that dramatic conflict. There is another element that is extremely important for all theatre, and that is the synthetic element. We synthesize and it unifies. We must all come to some kind of unity here for the very sake of unity. We will all go and do what we will when we leave this room. If we can come to some kind of unity, it is good. There is only one answer; there is really only one of anything. In terms of human action as we read it in our life in San Juan and I speak for us, there is one principle that everyone here is talking about that is more productive, more artistic, more just, more beautiful, more good all the time — to think of others first. It is a child's truth. Think of others first and you will get whatever you want. Do for others first, and you will achieve your dreams. Do for others and the world is yours. If some of us get angry and disturbed because we see people around us that don't do for others, that doesn't take away from the simplicity of the fact that we wish everyone would do — no matter how big the institution, no matter how complex the economics or what the problems are, if we don't sacrifice that fact, we have the answer, we have the talent, we have the justice we are seeking, and we can all die very well.

Some months later, looking back, Richard Schechner could take an affirmative position on FACT. He had not given up his conviction that the Broadway producer system was doomed. He had not changed his opinion of the basic motivation behind the commercial theatre's sponsorship of the conference. Out of it all, however, Schechner felt, "We did get a glimpse of a theatrical community across the country . . . During the Congress the community became identified with itself — it became a community even if it is a warring community." The confrontation in the end had been good. "It is better to have these differences among ourselves than with outside interests."

To a figure in the commercial theatre such as Gerald Schoenfeld, built-up hostilities were dispelled allowing a larger idea of theatre to emerge — a belief that more could be done collectively than individually. For himself, Schoenfeld had decided no longer to be passive about aspects of the theatre that were not his direct concern. The health of the organism as a whole depended on an enveloping soundness.

Hazel Bryant was eager to accept what help stronger forces could offer. Luis Valdez talked of synthesis and unity. Gilbert Moses hoped one outcome of FACT might be an understanding of the importance of the ethnic minority theatre. In the end, more people at the Congress wanted to preserve than to destroy, more people wanted to unify than divide. More people wanted to defend the right of everyone to be heard — free expression for all impartially — than wished for the destruction of those with whom they could not agree.

V. Profit and Non-profit:
Shared Problems and
Common Opportunities

In bringing together in one room the two realms of theatre — profit and non-profit — FACT opened the way to an important accommodation. If the panel on Alternative Theatre tended at first to polarize the two groups into warring camps, the panel on Stimulating Creative Resources acted to bring them together. One important outcome was the agreement in this panel to promote greater mobility of scripts and productions throughout the whole of the theatre.

The two realms of theatre in any case were becoming confused, one with the other, and sometimes they were indistinguishable. The profit-making or commercial theatre was no longer making very much of a profit. Certainly there were exceptions, and the rare hit could still prove to be immensely rewarding to a very lucky investor. But Bernard Jacobs had said that there was no future for the profit theatre "as we know it," and Richard Barr had said that for a *serious* play there was no longer any hope of profit on Broadway. In spite of the qualifications, these statements were ample recognition that the situation had changed vastly in only a few years.

From the non-profit side as well, lines of demarcation were becoming blurred. Non-profit institutions transferred their best productions to the commercial arena and operated in the big cultural centers in theatres that were as large and certainly as opulent as most theatres on Broadway. It was Gerald Schoenfeld who pointed out that, for all practical purposes, there was very little difference between a first-class production on Broadway and a first-class non-profit production in the Eisenhower Theatre of the Kennedy Center in Washington or the Vivian Beaumont Theatre in Lincoln Center in New York.

In each case, the same unions had jurisdiction and identical negotiations were required. To be sure, the playwright and the director might have financial arrangements different from those of their counterparts in the commercial theatre, to compensate for booking periods in the cultural centers that were limited and not open-ended as on Broadway. But almost every other contractual arrangement was the same for both kinds of productions. Even the ticket price scales were comparable, and the advertising displays in the newspapers were equivalent in size.

When Joseph Papp transferred four shows to Broadway, he found himself obliged to secure the services of a Broadway management office, and that same office handled his productions at Lincoln Center. In both places he had all the needs (except for investors) and worries of a commercial producer. "We worried about the grosses," Papp said. "We started reading Variety, which I never did before. You deal with unions and say we don't want sixteen musicians, but they say we do. So we negotiate with unions in the same way. We are dealing with budgets in the same way."

What made it possible for Papp to infiltrate the profit area was the vacuum at the center and the absence of quality material — but also the enormous and rapid expansion of his own resources. The biggest change that had come over the theatre in the last decade or so had been in where and how new plays originated. Throughout the 1940's and 1950's most new plays were born full-blown on Broadway. Broadway was the only incubator. In the 1960's some new work originated Off Broadway, and new playwrights developed there, cutting their teeth on the one-act play form. But now most new work asserts itself in a variety of new situations — in regional theatres, neighborhood theatres, black theatres, workshops and experimental theatres, universities. There has been a radical shift in the creative focal center of the theatre. As Lloyd Richards said when he moderated the panel on Stimulating Creative Resources:

"Whether we recognize it or not, there has been a fantastic evolution and revolution in the processes, the presentation form, and the means even of supporting theatre in this country."

Ruth Mayleas, of the National Endowment for the Arts, said their count of new plays done by resident professional theatre companies in the 1972-'73 season was 70. In some cases, college and university facilities have been utilized for the origination of new work. For example, Roger L. Stevens, of the Kennedy Center, had started off a production at the University of Tennessee in Knoxville. But academic associations often produce special difficulties. One drawback was a balancing requirement that a percentage of the students be involved in the production. Within the university environment such a *quid pro quo* might be an acceptable arrangement, but not if the production moved on commercially with students still in the cast.

The panel on Stimulating Creative Resources was set up to cope with such questions and other hinderances to the mobility of scripts and productions throughout the theatre system. It was concerned with two sorts of mobility — vertical and lateral: moving a play up to Broadway and moving a play across the country from one regional theatre to another. The technical problems were different in each case, but both implied some sort of public subsidy.

Subsidy was required to assure vertical movement because, as Richard Barr had pointed out, serious work could no longer make a profit on Broadway and investor interest was drying up. Barr and others remained convinced nevertheless that Broadway was the central arena, that regional theatres might successfully launch new work but be unable, even with occasional exposure on national television, to focus and centralize attention on the work in the way that Broadway was still capable of doing. He assumed, furthermore, that easier access to Broadway would stimulate production outside Broadway, a belief based on his own experience in the non-profit developmental area previous to his presidency of the League of New York Theatres and Producers. With his partners, Edward Albee and Clinton Wilder, utilizing some of the profits of their successful production of Albee's *Who's Afraid of Virginia Woolf?*, he had set up the Playwrights Unit in an Off Broadway theatre in 1963 to give new plays professional attention before invited audiences. In its six years of activity this project made possible the production of 85 plays.*

"Mostly it worked," Barr said, "because we got a hell of a lot of plays because we were producing uptown and at the Cherry Lane at the same time. Otherwise we wouldn't have gotten all those plays."

Barr proposed that a fund be set up to facilitate the transfer of worthwhile plays from the non-profit sector to Broadway. A model for the plan is in the making in Britain. Recognizing the scarcity of good dramatic material and the strong competition from television, the British Arts Council has established the Theatre Investment Fund as a potential pool of capital from which producing managements could draw or borrow in proportion to their own investment in the production; loans could equal but not exceed half the needed capital. The initial capitalization of the quasi-public fund will come partly through the Arts Council and partly through private subscription. Besides encouraging new plays and revivals of quality, the fund aims to encourage provincial tours and would participate in the profits and subsidiary rights of the productions it backs.

Barr's own proposal differs from this in stipulating that the transfer be accomplished on a non-profit basis throughout. Suppose a regional theatre had a new play and wanted the additional exposure of Broadway or Off Broadway. The theatre management would enter into an agreement with an experienced Broadway or Off Broadway producer – the

---

* At least two of which, *Dutchman* by LeRoi Jones and *The Boys in the Band* by Mart Crowley, became commercial successes.

choice under Barr's plan would be left to the playwright – to represent them and provide the expertise necessary in the complex marketplace of Broadway. This producer would then apply to the fund for financing. Some selection mechanism such as the Play Approval Committee of the Theatre Development Fund would be used to screen each application. Barr calculated that certain savings could be realized due to an already rehearsed cast, existing costumes, and a possibly reusable set. A Broadway mounting therefore might require no more than $75,000 instead of the usual $175,000 or $200,000 and an Off Broadway mounting $30,000 instead of $50,000. The originating theatre would receive a percentage of the profit. The playwright would earn his normal royalty. The rest of the profit would revert to the fund. For his services the producer would receive office expenses and either a flat fee or a percentage of the gross. The play would begin non-profit and end non-profit.

As moderator of the panel on Stimulating Creative Resources, Lloyd Richards was willing to postpone the working out of details, such as whether a whole new organization should be established for the purpose or whether an existing service group such as the Theatre Development Fund could be utilized. It was enough, he felt, for the panel to affirm its support for the idea in the hope thereby of making vertical mobility a recurring reality.

More important than getting the play to Broadway, in the judgment of Gordon Davidson, among others, was seeing that a play could more easily be handed around among the qualified resident professional theatres. Davidson argued for a notion he called "simultaneous quality." In other forms of entertainment, especially film, television, and popular music – alike in their special attraction for youth – the instant and widespread availability of the material was an important factor. In a colloquy with Joseph Papp, Davidson had said, "The only area you and I have really tangled on is when we have both been interested in a play and that play was not made available because of the marketplace conditions [and] the play only became available after you had done it."

Davidson wanted the ability to produce the play at the psychologically right moment for the work in question and at the right moment for its potential audience, regardless of whether someone else was also doing the play at the same time. Throughout the resident professional theatre system, rare though it might be for two theatres to be attracted simultaneously to the same script, the desire for a freer and less restrictive circulation of new plays was spreading. Being forced to wait a year or two for the rights to a new work to become available seemed to make less and less sense, even taking into full account the business interests of the originating producer. The Broadway system was based on exclusivity and unavailability. But deeply held as those articles of faith might be, weren't they now self-defeating? What was the real value and importance of reserving the rights to a possible road tour of a play that initially, as Richard Barr pointed out, might be incapable even of making a profit on Broadway? In short, measures preserving the old road system no longer seemed valid. And even if a road tour for a serious Broadway play were feasible, how, really, could such a tour be jeopardized by single productions of that play in the resident theatres of non-competing cities?

The panel also considered evidence that the resident theatres themselves were adopting some of the restrictive practices of the commercial theatre. Ever since *The Great White Hope* became a success on Broadway, resident professional theatres and other originating groups have been careful in their contracts with authors to reserve an interest in any subsequent commercial production of the play. In 1968 the Howard Sackler play, which starred James Earl Jones and Jane Alexander, moved from the Arena Stage in Washington to Broadway, under the commercial sponsorship of a Broadway producer. It became a hit, but in the absence of any special contractual provision no money went back to the Arena, which had supported the playwright and developed the play over a work period of many months. The Arena, in common with other resident professional theatres, had, of course, received public funding just to encourage new playwrights and develop such productions. Even so, it seemed right that a theatre should benefit materially from any windfall profits traceable to its efforts. Such money would go toward the encouragement of other playwrights and other plays. Unfortunately, if such an arrangement was pressed, it was the playwright who was most likely to suffer. A commercial producer, in offering the playwright a Broadway production, might require him to absorb, out of his royalty, the percentage the originating theatre now demanded.

The Barr proposal would circumvent this possibility in the case of a Broadway production. But it carried a potential hazard to a playwright should the play be circulated among the resident theatres themselves. Ruth Mayleas noted that new plays are increasingly being done in duplicate or in second productions by the regional theatres. The panel was told that sometimes three regional theatres could be found demanding percentages of the same play. The fortunate playwright whose work was wanted simultaneously by Zelda Fichandler, of the Arena Stage, Gordon Davidson, of the Mark Taper Forum, and Arvin Brown, of the Long Wharf in New Haven — unlikely though that might be — faced a difficult decision. Why could he not accept all and still earn his full royalty on each? Sometimes a well known playwright dealing with a lesser regional theatre can dictate the terms. More often, it is the theatre that will set the terms, by virtue of offering the opportunity of a production to an unknown playwright.

"I would be happy to be the first," said Gordon Davidson, "to give up any sense of claim on the playwright or anyone else, in terms of chattel or ownership or anything like that, because I resent the idea and abhor it. If one could find a way to create a new system of financing for the theatre as an art form, which would apply to all of us, so that we did not have to in any way put a lien on a playwright's income."

Again, there was a British precedent. The British Arts Council had once adopted a formula for subsidizing new plays in non-profit theatre companies. It guaranteed to make up the difference between the average box-office receipts as computed for six of the theatre's regular repertory productions and, if lower, the receipts of the new play. Thus, if six regular productions averaged out at 80 per cent of capacity and the new play fell to 60 per cent, the Arts Council would make up the difference in receipts.

Speaking for the panel, Lloyd Richards announced its recommendation that a new form of subsidy for the non-profit theatre be applied specifically to the playwright, so that he would in no way be deprived of his rights when a new play of promise was being developed.

From the floor came the query as to where such subsidy was to be found. Richards replied that the panel could not articulate the formula, only the principle. He said: "If we could, as a panel and as a group, express our concern for the percentage of the playwright's share of work that has been an impediment to the proliferation of that work and [our concern] that something be done in that regard, that may be as far as we can go."

Finally, the panel dealt directly with several sensitive union matters. The first was Equity's Showcase Code governing the relationships of its members with the Off Off Broadway and experimental theatre groups. Equity stipulates that if a showcase production is moved into a commercial situation the original actors are to be reused or else compensated. The rate of compensation is presently fixed at two weeks' pay, with additional considerations if the production goes into film or television. In theory, this appears to make good sense. Very often those actors have donated their services, both in rehearsal and in performance, in the interests of proving the work in question, as well as promoting their own employment. In practice, a potential commercial producer seeing the work may be attracted to the play, but not to the performances, and will not wish to be committed to every detail of the original production. The panel took the position: "This is a restriction against an author which is unfair to the author."

But there was a second matter, even more restrictive of the kind of mobility the panel wished to further between the non-profit and profit theatre. Many experimental, developmental, and ethnic theatres that depended on year-round company employment operated outside Equity because, economically, they could not exist if they accepted Equity standards of remuneration. Yet they were prevented from touring in theatres operated under Equity contracts. This barred them effectively from the resident professional theatres, the natural hosts to such groups in their home cities. "The New York environment can sustain all kinds of theatre," said Gordon Davidson, "and it is very important on the national scene that we also have similar possibilities."

The panel took the following stand, as expressed by Richards: "This body is concerned that non-Equity theatres be provided with a flexible mobility in relation to the touring of their work."

Ironically, it was only when performing outside of New York that such groups were ever able to make any money.

VI. What the Theatre Can Do for Itself

Every theatre's first responsibility is, of course, to the quality of what it presents on the stage. Good work has the miraculous property of easing the most stubborn peripheral problem. The uncertainty of financing or the reluctance of public support, the recalcitrance of the audience or the physical deterioration of the theatre district – these worries seem to vanish before the power of a strong dramatic work. As Marshall W. Mason told the panel on Stimulating Creative Resources, "If we create good theatre, we will have created a good business."

Mason is the artistic director of Circle Repertory, an Off Off Broadway group which had seen three new plays* become Off Broadway commercial successes. "We have to find new solutions to the central artistic problems," he said, "and in finding new solutions, there aren't any. It is a matter of reexamining what has worked in the past." For Mason, the old idea of a company was the most congenial solution. He said:

"A company is central in terms of continuity and in terms of developing relationships between playwrights and actors and directors."

For an academician such as Robert Brustein, dean of the Yale School of Drama, one answer was to subsidize the playwright within a learning situation; produce his play,

---

* Hot l Baltimore, When You Comin' Back, Red Ryder?, The Sea Horse.

allow him to associate with student playwrights, and let his experience "rub off" on them. At Yale this was made possible by an annual grant of $100,000 by the CBS Foundation to sponsor four playwright fellowships, a third of the money going directly to the playwrights, and the rest to the production costs of their plays.

For a pragmatist such as Joseph Papp, academic instruction and criticism for a playwright were mischievous. All that mattered was giving him a production.

> I am entirely opposed to institutionalized opportunities for criticism and instruction. If you want to kill anybody, do that. That should come out of the creative work and the process of work and not be separated in a kind of laboratory situation unless it relates to experimental work that has to do with workshop.
>
> There is no more effective way of stimulating a play-wright than by putting his play on and giving him an audience.

Similarly, Richard Barr expressed skepticism over the developmental possibilities for playwrights. "No playwright of interest or importance that I have ever produced has not come ready and full-blown. They are there, do not have to have workshops, do not have to have training. I agree that they have to have an opportunity to put a play on, but the whole idea that a playwright *develops* is erroneous."

If one accepts the judgment of such professionals as Mason, Brustein, Papp, and Barr, the theatre can best assist the playwright, not by intervention in his work processes, but by offering him a forum and assuring him of an audience. This implies the development of those essentials of theatrical planning and management that are concerned with technology, marketing, promotion, and audience building, which were the subjects of some of the more specialized FACT panels. All are aspects of the theatre's ability to help itself, quite apart from the separate and necessary benefits that might come from subsidy, ameliorative legislation, or other outside assistance.

Technology has to do with the delivery system — the

planning and design of new theatre buildings and the perfection of backstage equipment and techniques. The panel on technological developments learned that many theatres of the future, which must look to an effective life extending at least 25 years hence, will be multi-purpose houses. By means of quickly changeable and adaptable auditoriums the various performing arts can be accommodated and coexist — as in an auditorium that by turn is a 1,500-seat opera house, a 750-seat theatre for dramatic production, a 500-seat recital hall for music and dance, and a fourth plan with no fixed capacity, for experimental staging.

The designer George Izenour described another multiple-use house in Akron, Ohio: a 300-seat concert hall, which can turn into a 2,400-seat opera house, which can turn into a 900-seat dramatic theatre. Each fully automated shift can be accomplished in fifteen minutes. The main drawback of such theatres is that they preclude repertory companies with their specialized requirements for space and storage.

As a key principle of theatre design, Izenour laid down the requirement that the people on the spot — those who would be responsible for the theatre and those who would run it artistically — come to a complete agreement on the program of use well before the architect is brought in. A theatre could not be designed by committee, but neither could the architect write the program.

"Most people who build theatres," Izenour said, "do not understand what it is they want to build before they build. There is more lost motion, lost money, lost time, and lost effort by people indulging in the fantasies of architecture, who do not understand what it is they are trying to accomplish."

At the same time Izenour argued for the utilization of suitable existing facilities before a major commitment was made to proceed to new construction. "We Americans have the notion that the only thing that is good is something that is new. From an economic point of view, we can't keep this up, this knocking down of our architectural heritage — as sparse as it may be — and replacing it regularly every half-century. La Scala has been rebuilt three times."

In the redesign of the performing arts facilities of Milwaukee, in which Izenour was involved, a three-phase construction and redevelopment plan was devised. It included the construction of a 2,300-seat multiple-use facility for opera, concert, and recital; the resettlement of the Milwaukee Repertory Theatre, which, with its three-quarter-round staging, could not be integrated into a multiple-use facility; and the preservation and remodelling of the Pabst Theatre, a Milwaukee landmark. He had to fight for retention of the Pabst.

"I made the statement before the City Council," said Izenour, "that for Milwaukee to tear down the Pabst was like the Greek government trying to redevelop the Acropolis."

Reclaimed, the Pabst would be suitable for first-class touring companies and musicals and would ideally supplement the other facilities.

The new theatre technologies — at their best in the development of such multiple-purpose buildings and in readapting standing structures like the Pabst to new uses — were not in themselves miracle cures for what Dr. Baumol called the "cost disease" afflicting all the performing arts, extending even to modern culture centers. There were, to be sure, synchronous winches backstage for the rigging; computerized lighting control systems, handled from pre-set lighting boards, that worked brilliantly; and pneumatic lifts capable of raising four-foot modules of a stage floor in six-inch increments. But when Dr. Baumol inquired as to how much such new technologies could be expected to shave off costs of operation, the answer was disappointing.

First of all, qualified manpower capable of running a permanently installed complex rigging system or a computerized lighting system were hard to find and commanded high pay. Unions opposed them anyway because they precluded the make-work opportunities of the move-in and the move-out. Furthermore, as designer Ralph Alswang pointed out, no two lighting designers could agree on the placement of the equipment.

Even where theatres have the required equipment in place, a new show will insist on installing its own lighting board and having its own complete rigging system flown. As Dr. Baumol had warned, the very nature of live performance, where costumes, sets, and lighting are all custom-made, permits little increase in productivity even when the technology is available.

And Izenour observed:

"It is impossible to make an art form efficient. The theatre cannot be made efficient in terms of an industry. You can have all the machinery in the world, and you are not going to facilitate the expression of the essential artistic idea."

If technological progress offered only limited help to the theatre, there was more promise in developing better techniques of audience building, marketing, and promotion. The need always to be doing something about increasing the size of the audience is self-evident. In the commercial theatre costs have gone up so steeply that a Broadway show has to run longer to break even. "We are attracting as many people as we did before but we need more people," said Bernard Jacobs.

The panel on The Audience for the Theatre Today agreed that insufficient attention had been paid to the enormous changes in audience composition over the last 50 years. Statistical evidence is scarce and difficult to produce. The panel was to have the benefit of a significant, broadly applicable audience survey brought from Minneapolis by Bradley G. Morison. There was, in addition, ample evidence in the testimony of a variety of delegates that new theatres and new theatre ideas have created new audiences.

Woodie King, Jr., of the New Federal Theatre at the Henry Street Settlement, stressed the role of black theatre in revitalizing the whole theatre movement in New York. Black theatres have developed their own constituencies in the neighborhoods, but have also stimulated the movement of black plays to Off Broadway, Broadway, and Lincoln Center. In the 1970's black audiences began to patronize Broadway in significant numbers for the first time. It was Hazel Bryant who pointed out that it wasn't only to the rich white that richly decorated theatres appealed; the appreciation of less fortunate blacks for fine theatres and luxurious public places was all the greater for the drabness of their own homes and living conditions.

The New York theatre, whose response to the great ethnic changes taking place in the city may have been inadequate, was nevertheless discovering many sorts of new audiences. There was good evidence that new audiences for theatre were created by the Times Square Ticket Center [TKTS]. As an experiment in marketing, the center was established by the Theatre Development Fund in June, 1973, to sell theatre tickets at half price (plus a small service charge) on the day of performance only. TKTS, receiving allotments of unsold tickets from participating theatres, acted as a central box office for Broadway, Off Broadway, Lincoln Center, City Center, the Brooklyn Academy of Music, and other institutions. Surveys showed that many of its sales were made to persons who were not accustomed to attending the theatre. And the majority of tickets were sold to impulse buyers who made plans to attend no more than two days before performance. Among the TKTS patrons was a higher share of less affluent professional and blue collar workers than one usually finds among regular Broadway theatregoers. From the data available there was a strong presumption that in large part TKTS was bringing wholly new categories of theatregoers to Broadway.

TKTS is undoubtedly the most important marketing innovation in the New York theatre since the introduction of the credit card by American Express and Ticketron, which simplified and decentralized ticket-buying procedures. American Express has six million credit card holders paying $20 a year for its privileges, and 55 per cent of them are on record as having a vital and active interest in the performing arts. The card was first introduced in 1970 and has been accepted by virtually the whole of Broadway and many Off Broadway theatres. For the service, the theatres pay a percentage on gross volume that does not exceed six per cent; but since 1973, according to Robert H. Leach, an American Express vice president who participated in the FACT panel on marketing, most of the money earned in this way has been plowed back into the theatre in an extensive advertising and promotion campaign.

The use of a telephone reservation system in conjunction with the card, operating since spring, 1974, has increased business significantly. The theatre is obliged to state the seat locations and the limitations on pick-up — no less than a half hour before curtain. American Express does not guarantee sales but the no-shows are said to be minimal. When American Express began promotion of the phone service, business quadrupled.

Ticketron represents computer technology adapted to the marketing of entertainment tickets. It has more application to major sports events and popular rock concerts than it does to theatre, to which it first came, in a small way, in 1967. Howard Erskine, of Ticketron, described selling out an entire three-performance appearance of The Who at the Nassau Coliseum on Long Island — a total of 45,000 seats — in 31 minutes. Operating nationwide, Ticketron draws upon two computers, one in California and the other in New Jersey. With a few exceptions, due to holdout theatres, it receives allotments that average about 120 tickets per theatre for most Broadway performances. They go on sale at the 131 terminals in the greater New York area, including those in major department stores. The customer has an opportunity to check locations and receives a print-out ticket on the spot, paying a premium for the service. On the night before performance the computer will close down business, and a full report of tickets sold will be in the hands of the theatre treasurer in the morning. As a marketing tool to pinpoint advertising effectiveness, this report can also provide the time and place of sale.

FACT considered a number of other marketing innovations

in theatre — limited in scope compared to TKTS, American Express, and Ticketron, yet in applicability equally significant, possibly more so for being tailored to the theatre's special requirements. Dr. Baumol described the Theatre Development Fund's voucher as a new tool to subsidize both audience and theatre at the same time. The voucher is a packet of five admission slips made available at a purchase price of $5 to a TDF list of teachers, students, union members, retired persons and others. Each is worth $2.50 toward admission to any qualifying Off Off Broadway theatre on TDF's list and is redeemable at TDF for that amount. The margin of subsidy is therefore the difference between the $5 purchase price and the $12.50 redeemable value. The voucher, Dr. Baumol noted, brought retired people as well as young people to Off Off Broadway performances and demonstrably created new audiences for that branch of theatre. It also encouraged those theatres to utilize TDF mailing lists and solicit special groups.

The FACT panel on Innovations in Marketing decided on the shared need of both the commercial and the non-profit theatre for a comprehensive study of more productive marketing and promotional techniques. The implementation of such measures would mean revising habits of long standing and dropping customs to which the commercial theatre in particular held tenaciously. Broadway, for example, was still caught up in selling a show, rather than a season, or Broadway itself as an institution. A number of panel speakers suggested that it was time to abandon the individualistic approach in favor of cooperative action — the use of joint mailing lists, institutional advertising, and so forth. Television, which had been so successfully employed by popular musicals in recent seasons, presented itself as a promising advertising medium supplementing if not supplanting newspapers. An ex-Broadway press agent, Harvey Sabinson, advanced the radical notion that the way to reach the public anyway was not through time-honored campaigns to place self-serving paragraphs in the paper but by working within the community. More important than the catchy press release were new ways to market the theatre ticket. The press agent, he suggested, might more usefully function as a community relations director. That was a metamorphosis that had already taken place rather widely among the resident professional theatre groups. Jon Jory, of the Actors Theatre of Louisville, said theatre should sell not a product but a process to the community, involving them, as their skills and interests allowed, in such functions as costume-making or set building. The panel agreed on a need for national seminars, for directors of community relations, to accomplish a sharing of these techniques.

James B. McKenzie, out of his experience as executive producer of the American Conservatory Theatre in San Francisco, suggested a clean sweep of some ancient taboos and customs: dropping the elitism of opening nights and of V.I.P. seats and special treatment, placing less reliance on critic-quote ads, reducing the dominance of theatre parties, eliminating the star system, instituting a mandatory student rush, forbidding the sale of high-price souvenir programs in the lobby, abandoning the no-refund ticket policy. His suggestions were calculated to de-emphasize the social prestige appeal in theatregoing and make it a more ordinary and necessary activity of the people.

Individual theatres had other audiences and other programs. A theatre such as the Off-Broadway Roundabout built subscription very rapidly with its classic repertory policy and attracted, it was said, the sort of audience the Theatre Guild had on Broadway in the 1930's and 1940's. The New York Shakespeare Festival dealt with multiple audiences that were by no means overlapping. Those who lined up for free Shakespeare in Central Park differed from the "unmotivated" audiences who watched theatre when the mobile stage visited their neighborhoods, and differed still more from the mostly middle-aged Public Theatre passholders who bought the season's events before they were announced. The Festival's uptown audience at Lincoln Center, which included a large subscription list inherited from the previous management of the Vivian Beaumont Theatre, had little in common with the Festival's other constituencies. The Chelsea in Brooklyn, as a matter of policy, abjured the use of cut rates and bargains to lure subscribers. It relied instead on a following that was 70 per cent local and loyally committed itself to the body of work done by the Chelsea rather than being attracted to individual plays as they were announced.

In much this manner, by encouraging loyalty and pride in the institution, the major resident professional theatres across the country had built their patronage, and it was this growing body of theatregoers that constituted the most significant new American theatre audience. One such audience, that of the Tyrone Guthrie Theatre in Minneapolis, was subjected to a ten-year research study to determine the cumulative effects of promotion, public relations, and educational programs on the size and composition of the audience. It was that study, and its rather surprising findings, that Mr. Morison reported to the FACT panel on Audience.

By means of sophisticated marketing research techniques and an audience sample of 10,000, a profile of the Guthrie audience was taken in its first season in 1963. It was repeated 10 seasons later, in 1973, after $1.5 million was spent in various kinds of promotion and audience development work. The Minneapolis researchers were startled by the results. Except in one important respect, the Guthrie audience had not changed materially either in demographic characteristics or in frequency of attendance. In 1963, the proportion of the population in the Guthrie's market area which attended one or more plays amounted to 2.10 per cent. In 1973, the figure was 2.13 per cent — an increase of less than two per cent. With all the national and local attention focussed on the Guthrie opening in 1963 it was understandable, perhaps, that attendance had started at a very high level. But over 11 seasons the increase was only a little more than the increase in the local population. Most of the other comparisons in the survey were similarly close despite the 10-season spread.

The exception was significant. The one important change

was a drop in the median age of the audience from 35 years in 1963 to 30 years in 1973. In 1973, 60 per cent of the audience was under 36 years of age. In the 1963 season about 18 per cent of the audience fell in the 18-25 age range. By 1973 it had increased to 28 per cent of the total audience. Allowing for the natural decrease in the median age of the population, this amounted to a real increase in the number of young people individually attending regular performances. Projected, this trend meant the Guthrie could have a real increase in total audience of 15 to 20 per cent in the next ten years as contrasted to the less than two per cent in the first ten years.

How to explain this increase? From its first season the Guthrie made a practice of special matinees for high and junior high school students. There were accompanying background and study materials, workshops, demonstrations, and talks. Here was hard evidence that a student program works. There was another factor. Along with the Guthrie, Minneapolis also had the benefit of an exceptional children's theatre under the direction of John Clark Donahue for which a new $5 million theatre and school have been built. The combination of these two influences gave the young people of Minneapolis extraordinary exposure to a range of good theatre. The evidence of the parallel surveys forced Morison to conclude:

> First, that the application of money and professional talent to extensive and basically sound marketing, advertising, promotion and publicity does not substantially change the size or nature of an audience for a theatre.
>
> Second, that imaginative programs for introducing young people to the theatre and the opportunity for young people to see a variety of good theatre on a consistent basis from the earliest age on *do* build larger audiences for theatre.

Morison felt, therefore, that the professional theatre itself could no longer afford to ignore a responsibility to introduce young people to good theatre. He recommended that an institute and laboratory be established to examine and experiment with the relationship between the performing arts and young people; that the National Endowment for the Arts give grants to poets, playwrights, and musical writers to create works specifically for the young; and that producers and theatres agree to mount at least one production each season especially for young audiences.

For the experience of Minneapolis taught that in the cultivation of young theatregoers an expanding theatre could best prepare the ground for new audiences.

VII. Public and Private Support for Theatre

However much the theatre might wish to be self-support-
ing, it is forced more and more to rely on outside help. This
means going back again and again to the reliable and proven
sources of assistance. It means finding new sources and
finding new ways to get more out of the old sources.

The way the New York State Council on the Arts managed
to achieve an extraordinary high level of funding is an object
lesson in the value of developing research data to justify a
request. Certainly great credit for the $34.1 million appro-
priated in New York for 1974-'75 (and repeated the
following year) was due to a governor friendly to the arts,
Nelson A. Rockefeller. But this record government appropria-
tion might not have been possible at all without the
groundwork laid in prior years by the state Cultural
Resources Commission under the chairmanship of State
Senator William T. Conklin. Speaking to a FACT panel,
Senator Conklin recalled how the commission, by canvassing
the state, had dug out the figures on the visual and
performing arts: union employment of 33,000; public attendance of 71 million; box office receipts of $300 million;
capital assets of $6 billion. With this evidence of economic
impact Senator Conklin succeeded in persuading many
skeptical and scoffing legislators to back the arts with
substantial state funds.

The influence of government on the theatre of the 1970's is
pervasive — as patron, tax collector, regulator, and sometimes
contractor of services. With the help of legislators and other

government officials, as well as theatre lawyers and experts, FACT examined these multiple relationships in some detail, determining where the obstacles as well as the openings were. Congressman Edward I. Koch of New York held out small hope for suggested changes in the tax laws affecting theatrical investment. One could argue, of course, that the commercial theatre, while concentrated in Manhattan, was in reality a national resource deserving of special consideration. Yet writing tax concessions into legislation that would affect primarily New York investors and New York productions smacks of the special interest bill. Congressman Koch told FACT: "I believe that, along with others, I am able to get other members of Congress interested in such a program if you can show them two things: if you can show them that the whole country benefits, and if you can show them that some area they are very familiar with benefits."

Representing the theatre district, Congressman Koch offered to cooperate with any working staff established by FACT to help develop reasonable and possible legislative programs. But he was quick to admit that he might not be the best placed person to help. Knowing who the key legislators are on the controlling committees would require the attention of a full-time lobbyist, as was pointed out by Jack Golodner, a Washington attorney who specializes in arts consultation. To influence legislation before it was too late, one had to keep track of what was coming up before Congress that might affect the theatre and know who was most directly concerned, in order to concentrate the right attention on the right person at the right time.

Again, research data was needed in support of legislative action. Much of it was available through the government, in the files of the National Endowment, in the census figures, and in accumulations of data in various theatre service organizations such as the Theatre Communications Group, the unions, and the different theatre leagues. But such data needed to be accumulated, organized, and disseminated from a central source to support the theatre's appeals for public help.

FACT panels considered tax reform in various categories: tax incentives to encourage investment in the commercial theatre, the removal of excise taxes, the lifting of taxes from various operations of the non-profit theatre. A poll conducted by Thomas Fichandler, of the Arena Stage in Washington, revealed that out of 26 members of the League of Resident Theatres, 12 were subject to sales or admissions taxes — some paying city taxes, some state, and some both. The Arena itself was in the curious position of receiving government funding from the National Endowment on the one hand while being taxed on admissions by the District of Columbia on the other, so that for every Federal dollar given out the district took away 50 cents. In the poll, six out of 25 theatres reported paying real estate taxes.

In order to attract more investment capital into the commercial theatre, a number of tax incentive methods were discussed. One was an investment tax credit, modelled on the seven per cent credit granted to businesses, specifically to encourage investment in new machinery and equipment. Such a tax would allow investors to take a percentage of their investment as a deduction, in addition, of course, to any losses. Another method was to permit the sheltering of income in the manner of the oil depletion allowance. Just as some oil companies, holding what are considered to be wasting assets, are allowed to deduct 22 per cent of revenues off the top before the rest of the tax income is reported, so theatre investors, the value of whose investment decreases rapidly in time, should be allowed a similar concession.

An equivalent sheltering of the playwright's income was considered although such a concession brought up the question of tax preferment for all writers. Still, it should be noted that the theatre is one area of business that has received no beneficial tax legislation, except in the removal of the Federal admissions tax. A depreciation write-off allowance that is applicable to movie companies was disallowed to the theatre since it can show no tangible property, such as a can of film, but only the ephemeral product of the live performance.

While no one suggested the desirability of tax relief for a commercially run theatre building booked profitably, tax relief might be sought for such a theatre when dark, thereby helping to protect the character of the existing theatre district against the encroachments of outside real estate forces.

As a levy imposed for the benefit of the theatre, the San Francisco hotel tax was discussed pro and con. This tax amounts to seven per cent on hotel room sales, and its proceeds of a little more than $1 million a year help to fund the city's arts organizations. A dedicated tax, however, is not only the *source* of revenue but the *limit* of revenue. Philosophically as well as pragmatically, it seemed preferable for the arts to be given a place in the municipal budget, reviewable annually. The hotel tax had another drawback. It saddled the city and its arts industry with an inherited enemy — the visitors who had to pay double for diversions they might otherwise enthusiastically support.

Industry problems in theatre are so highly specialized and so completely lacking in parallels with those of other industries as to confound routine regulatory procedures of government, often to the detriment of the theatre. Few in the theatre would question the perfectly proper regulatory functions of the government. But theatre managers would like to be relieved to some of the unnecessary burdens of this regulation — the onerous delays caused by Securities and Exchange Commission [SEC] procedures governing the financing of commercial productions, for example, and the confusions caused by overlapping state and municipal regulations, notably in New York State. In each case the theatre would benefit immeasurably if knowledgeable persons were designated to handle the problems as they arose.

Time is often of the essence in coordinating the financing of a commercial production with such other elements as the availability of a theatre and the hiring of a director, designers, and actors. An interstate offering, under the limited partnership form of agreement used in the financing of Broadway shows, requires the filing of a registration statement with the SEC in Washington. Such statements are not always reviewed by the same person. Often a new official is brought in cold; a common approach is lacking, and delays result.

To some extent, this hazard can be circumvented under SEC's Regulation A, which applies to capitalizations under $500,000, and the filing can be accomplished through the regional office in New York where the reviewing officers are more familiar with the theatre's special problems. Better still, if the offering is restricted to 35 investors who are presumed to be sophisticated in the special risks of the commercial theatre, Rule 146 — a new rule promulgated by the SEC — applies, and then the filing of a prospectus is not required.

As for the situation in New York, Gerald Schoenfeld, who moderated the panel on Legislation Restricting the Professional Theatre, pointed out that separate state and city rules are overlapping, often archaic, and in some cases impractical. Through the New York State Theatrical Financing Law, the state regulates the sale of tickets, play financing, and the operations of brokers and of theatre box office personnel. The law is administered by the State Attorney General. Separate city regulations covering some of the same ground are administered by the Department of Consumer Affairs. It would be helpful, Schoenfeld suggested, if only one set of laws applied and if one governmental body, run by a person who was familiar with the theatre's special problems, was in charge.

Finally, Schoenfeld called for repeal of the real estate tax on theatre and of other nuisance taxes. The saving to the theatre could be put to good advantage on a number of promising and needed projects such as the physical improvement of the theatre district, the computerization of ticket sales, and special research studies to help the theatre.

Regulatory matters aside, the theatre and government are thrown into closest relationship in the struggle to restore and preserve the urban environment. As Broadway has a stake in Times Square, so theatres in cities across the country are dependent upon the vigor of downtown life and align themselves with like-minded civic groups to seek results at the local government level.

The wave of new building everywhere has crested. For reasons of economic necessity, if not for sensible preservation sentiments, Americans are being jarred out of spendthrift "disposable culture" attitudes which have allowed fine old buildings to be discarded, neighborhoods destroyed, and dehumanizing office towers of concrete and glass to be erected in their place. There is fresh hope for the recycling of old buildings where the original purpose can be replaced with a modern use. In New York, imaginative planners were brought together under the Lindsay Administration to develop new ways to defend cultural values against the encroachments of commercial self-interest. Under the leadership of Donald H. Elliott of the City Planning Commission, an Urban Design Group was staffed with leading young architect-planners — William G. Bardel, Jacquelin T. Robertson, and Richard Weinstein, who fought for and won the power to trade off zoning restrictions for social advantage. After the uninhibited building boom in New York City which transformed first Third Avenue and then Sixth Avenue and threatened to explode next in Times Square, Lindsay's planners devised the Theatre District Code. If the coming of office towers threatened to make cruel anachronisms of the existing structures, scaled as they were to no higher than a proscenium arch, the city would use whatever muscle it had to ensure that theatres would be incorporated into the new buildings at ground level. The "incentive zoning" provisions of the code resulted in the construction of four new theatres in office buildings in the Times Square area. As Richard Weinstein told FACT, the first of these new theatres, the Minskoff in the W.T. Grant building, erected on the site of the old Astor Hotel, was the first example in the United States "of the effort to divert commercial activity into cultural ends and to find in the ordinary operation of our economy ways of funding the arts."

But there were drawbacks to the new scheme. Jerome

Minskoff told the FACT panel on Restoration of the Urban Environment that actual costs of operation and maintenance had proved to be much higher than estimated; he would not build another such theatre regardless of the zoning inducements offered by the city. That such costs would be critical, Weinstein said, his group recognized from the outset; there was a need to find a way to build relief from running costs into the plan. In the future, some scheme for the trade-off of air rights, which might allow small free-standing buildings such as legitimate theatres to remain on their valuable land by assigning their air rights elsewhere, could prove to be the best hope for the future of the theatre district.

Every construction and building change altered the population profile of the district. The replacement of hotels, restaurants, and theatres by office towers emptied at the end of the day meant a net depletion of the night population of the area. On a much smaller scale, the addition of the outdoor TKTS trailer to Times Square, as a sort of central box office, was especially valued by the city for bringing people back in. And the presence of these theatregoers was all the more welcome for being so visible as each afternoon and early evening, in warm weather and cold, they formed two lines on either side of the trailer in the small triangle at the head of the square where Father Duffy's statue stands.

The Times Square Ticket Center owes its form and shape to the convergent lines of interest of local, state, and Federal government, private foundations, and corporations, meeting on a single cultural need.

Moderating the panel on foundations, Stephen Benedict, then president of the Theatre Development Fund, a catalytic agent in this project as in other theatre ventures, said, "This Congress is structured in such a way as to break down the available and identifiable sources of assistance in the energy crisis that confronts the theatre, the fuel shortage if you will, into its component parts, of which the foundation world is an important one."

The Congress convened in the summer of 1974 — in the

midst of the downturn of the economy as intensified by the oil crisis, but before the sharpest fall of the stock market and consequently of the portfolio values of large foundations. By the time of the Congress, however, sail trimming on the part of the foundations was already apparent; the Rockefeller Foundation, for one, under new leadership, was altering course perceptibly at the expense of the arts. More important than the shift itself was the feared domino effect the Rockefeller retrenchment might have on other foundations, some of them already pulling in as government funding at both state and Federal levels expanded. Philosophically, foundations dedicated to broad problems of human welfare always questioned themselves as to how deep support for the arts should go.

Still, as Benedict indicated, there were a number of new opportunities for the theatre that members of the panel could consider; specifically, among a grand total of 25,000 foundations, the presence of many smaller foundations whose potential resources for theatre have gone virtually untapped. Benedict urged the panel to readjust its focus, to pull back from the larger, well-staffed foundations with defined programs and take a broader view of the possibilities. A wider base would then appear. Individual patronage still accounted for 70 per cent of the giving in the arts. Trust officers in banks controlled funds that represented another unexplored source. Foundation money could be used as leverage on the giving of corporations. As targets of persuasion there remained, first, the foundations that had never before given to the arts and, second, those that used to give but had stopped.

Public lobbying could well go unheeded by foundations, or have a negative effect, but a careful and sophisticated job of education should influence not only the funding officer but the trustees. The theatre was responsible for seeing that just the right informational inputs reached the deciding officials. Counter-argument was needed, for example, to repair the damage after a Louis Harris poll came out with a dismaying finding that 61 per cent of a sample of frequent attendees of cultural events, in all the arts, believed that professional theatre made money and that 78 per cent believed it made money or broke even. One could not assume that foundation trustees, unprompted, would supply their own corrective to these misapprehensions.

Foundations are understaffed for the complexity of the decisions they are called upon to make. Each foundation develops its own criteria for applications — the quantifying of a series of subjective judgments, in the phrase of one foundation executive. Emphasis falls on personnel, capabilities, program objectives, past record, and so forth, without enough attention, in the opinion of John E. Booth, one member of the foundation panel, to the artistic quality of the applying group. The proliferation of theatre organizations is such that individual evaluations of all applications are impossible, both in the larger foundations and in the National Endowment. "I might just as well blindfold myself and put my hand in a twirling basket," said Stephen Benedict of his project reviewing experience at the Rockefeller Brothers Fund. In such situations foundations would rather do business with service organizations, such as the Off Off Broadway Alliance (OOBA), than with the theatres themselves.

Each foundation has its own priorities, its internal debates over long-term commitments versus one-time grants, its soul-searching over the significance of the performing arts. Often the paperwork at the front end of an application is so arduous that little time is left for follow up. Fund-raising is a handicraft industry. No single set of criteria applies. To see if he qualifies, an applicant should take the trouble to read several annual reports to locate the areas of concentration of that foundation and review its history of giving. Once he becomes a recipient, George White, president of the Eugene O'Neill Memorial Theatre Center, suggested, the grantee would do well to report progress and fulfillment back to the donor foundation, and not be so secretive about his sources as to deny his colleagues in the field valuable data.

FACT recognized the need of smaller foundations, particularly, for some relief from the Tax Reform Act of 1969. That legislation was enacted in response to conservative fears that foundations had grown too big and were becoming too politically activist. By means of a graduated surtax on net investment income, it aimed to force out more grant payments, while also slowing the flow of new money into foundations and making new foundations more difficult to establish. It included prohibitions against political activity and subjected grants to individuals to special and cumbersome clearance procedures.

While aimed at the practices of larger foundations, the act had greater impact on smaller foundations, which lacked the staff and expertise to cope with the required paperwork. In 1969, a conservative Congress feared the unhealthy enlargement of the foundation universe. In 1974, after the stock market slide that eroded the investment portfolios of foundations by as much as a third, the situation was reversed. The ability of foundations to meet the swelling needs of their clients was endangered.

As a potential untapped source of funding, business corporations represented much the same sort of opportunity as did the many thousands of smaller foundations. Encouraged by the Business Committee for the Arts, a national organization, major corporations had significantly increased the level of giving in recent years. A greater potential remained. Corporations were not yet near the maximum 5 per cent write-off on pre-tax income allowable by the I.R.S. for contributions. Furthermore, the importance of corporate gifts to theatre rises in proportion to the fall in foundation support. Corporate earnings had been sustained at a high level despite the market slump. This made realistic the possibility of greater corporate gifts while the drop in the value of portfolios deprived the foundations of the opportunity to maintain their high level of giving. Uncounted in the totals of their giving, yet of real monetary value to the recipient, were the loaned or donated business equipment and the contributed executive skill provided by many companies.

If small foundations lacked the staff to process applications and evaluate requests, corporations were at an even greater disadvantage. An applying theatre usually had the best luck if it was able to reach the highest executive in the company, especially if he was interested in the arts and could be persuaded to become personally involved. If the request was for a specific project, such as one performance or one production, it was more usually referred to the public relations and advertising department, which generally required some promotional advantage such as company identification with the project.

Philosophically, most large corporations accepted the responsibility of community service. More practically, many had decided they could no longer remain vital and profitable without helping materially to improve the community in which they existed. For them the selling point was social service and not art, educational purpose rather than aesthetic value. FACT panel members advised theatres applying to corporate donors: Be precise as to program, budgets, who will execute the program, why it is needed, who will benefit, and so forth. Most theatres today are well trained by the periodic requirements of government agencies and foundations for audits and reports. They are able to meet the high expectations of corporations, which demand competence and fiscal sophistication in their business partners.

Sometimes appeals to business are best made on a consolidated basis. An example is the Lincoln Center Corporate Fund, as described to FACT by John W. Mazzola, managing director of Lincoln Center. With a gross annual operating budget of $70 million, Lincoln Center and all its constituents take in $49 million annually at the box office, leaving a deficit of $21 million that has to be accounted for out of government and foundation grants and individual and corporate gifts. Instead of having each constituent canvass corporate donors individually, the Center conducts a consolidated drive on an industry-by-industry basis: one knock on the corporate door instead of eight by the different constituents. By this means — as well as through the fortunate circumstance of having many leading corporation executives sitting on its various boards — Lincoln Center has been able to boost corporate giving from a level of $800,000 to $1.5 million.

The other side of the problem is how to get across to the business community the importance of the very small theatre which does not have the community visibility of Lincoln Center or a comparable opportunity to solicit support. How could business be made more aware of the needs and social significance of all theatre? The Congress considered an educational program equivalent in scope to the work done in New York State by Concerned Citizens for the Arts and nationally by the Partnership for the Arts. For FACT well recognized that the more money asked of corporations, the more would be available.

Less tangible than this sort of help, but scarcely less important to the theatre, was the recognition of press, radio, and television — important partly because it had such a direct bearing on financial support. Regional theatres, for example, eagerly sought national magazine and newspaper coverage, not because it was needed to attract audience but because it was the best way to draw the attention of the major funding organizations.

In theatre reportage and criticism, the discouragements and restraints had to do with the space shortcomings of magazines, the drop in the number of newspapers or the decrease in newspaper coverage, and the time limitations of television on which often no more than 60 to 90 seconds are devoted to a major review. Theatre is in competition with the other arts and entertainment, and they with all the other departments in the paper or on the television screen, and the departments with the news, in a continual scramble for preferment. The crucial mediators in these space and time battles are the editors, whose competence or interest in the arts is sometimes at question. Unremitting pressure must be brought to bear on them.

T.E. Kalem, of Time Magazine, said that editors placed

great stock in the incoming mail as an indicator of the interests of readers. Traditionally, at least in Time, theatre draws few letters to the editor. Grace Glueck, of The New York Times, pointed to the proliferation of dance in the past five or so years and the variety of performances that had caused excitement among an expanding audience for this form of entertainment. Such considerations forced the hand of the Times to increase dance coverage. Almost all the panelists agreed that the theatre could best make its case at the level of the editor or publisher; the critics and reporter specialists were among the already converted but were powerless to influence space allotments.

As for criticism, Peter Zeisler, director of the Theatre Communications Group and co-chairman of the FACT panel on Media, identified one current weakness as the failure to measure plays as "a manifestation of something within society." Very largely they are considered in a sterile isolation. Robert Brustein supported this view. He said he was less worried about space and whether the regional theatre was covered nationally than about the philosophical dependency of criticism on the commercial system of play producing.

> This means that the emphasis of the critic is automatically going to be on the individual play and the individuals in that play. They see part of their function as the economic support of the theatre, keeping it alive or killing it, but anyway establishing the hits or flops of the commercial theatre. They are geared toward the audience, telling them what to see, and they are not always as conscious as they should be about the theatre itself and its continuing organic development. In other words, we have repertory theatres but we don't have very many repertory critics.

Richard Schechner argued the existence of mutually exploitative relationships, the critics with the theatre and the theatre with the critics, and Marilyn Stasio, of Cue, suggested that theatre and critics both had been reduced to the status of commodities in the media culture.

What could free writers and critics of individual responsibility, according to Ernest Schier, of the Philadelphia Evening Bulletin, was a continuity of work that assured a degree of permanence. "When you have to deal with a resident company or a regional company or a series [of plays] provided by the same management, you know that it *is* going to happen. Your responsibility is no longer financial. You don't have to fuss around in your head as to whether it is economic or not."

Brustein felt that finally it was up to the government to free the theatre of its economic dependency on the press, but in his impromptu summation of the future of the theatre came a note of optimism as strong as any expressed at the Congress:

> I don't sense any falling off whatsoever in the theatre. On the contrary, I sense an important increase of enthusiasm and new commitment on the part particularly of young people in theatrical events. I have never seen that kind of one-to-one [relationship] with an audience or felt the kind of electric excitement out of an audience that I am beginning to experience in a number of places. It gives me a great deal of hope. I don't think it is dying at all. I couldn't believe more than I do at this moment that it is very strong and very alive.

VIII. Agenda for Action

The organizers of FACT recognized from their first meetings in the early fall of 1973 that the chief test of the success of the conference would be in whether the participants wished to see it repeated. Such a decision, and no more, would justify the time and energy expended. "If the Congress achieves what we think it will achieve," said Alexander H. Cohen in his opening remarks, "[a second Congress] will be the logical outcome. If it doesn't, it won't be worth repeating anyway."

As the Congress itself was drawing to a close the steering committee debated whether it should sponsor a resolution calling for a second FACT but decided to hold off and await events. In the final plenary session two resolutions were offered spontaneously from the floor. One, by Lloyd Richards, provided that a repeat Congress be held, and the other, by Marilyn Stasio, provided that the steering committee be retained and enlarged as an ongoing body to follow up on the work of the Congress and pursue suggested lines of action. Both resolutions were approved enthusiastically by the delegates.

Unanimity on broad matters was essential if FACT was to play an effective role in the future. At the closing banquet, Warren Caro, of the steering committee, alluded to the coincidence of FACT taking place in Princeton on the 200th anniversary of the First Continental Congress in Philadelphia. Common to both times and places was an urgency to achieve agreement for the sake of agreement. John Hancock had said in Philadelphia, "We must be unanimous; there must be no pulling different ways, we must all hang together." To which Benjamin Franklin replied, "We must hang together, or, most assuredly, we shall all hang separately."

FACT's own sense of urgency was conveyed in the Statement of Purpose drafted for the conference:

"No group with a direct stake in the future of the theatre can afford to abstain from the process of reexamination of the premises of theatrical organization and operation which this conference will launch. The issues are too important and the problems too pressing to permit postponement of common strategies for whose design this Conference will provide the forum."

Throughout the fall of 1974 and the winter of 1975 the carried-over steering committee, reorganized into a coordinating committee, met regularly to make the permanent arrangements for FACT. Initially, FACT would have a small office in New York and a number of working advisory committees whose assigned areas of responsibility would correspond to those of the panels at the Congress. The board met for long hours on the organization of these committees, on setting goals for them, and on the appointment to them of recognized national leaders from many areas — business, finance, foundations, and communications. The committee structure will operate as FACT's major means of enlisting the interest and assistance of the wider community.

Steps were taken to incorporate under the name of FACT as a not-for-profit corporation under the laws of New York State. The office was established in November on the fourth floor of 226 West 47th Street in New York — a building which houses other theatrical organizations including the League of New York Theatres and Producers, the Theatre Guild, and the production company of Richard Barr. The members of the coordinating committee, with some additions, became the board of directors of FACT. The additions, which included John E. Booth, associate director of the Twentieth Century Fund, Joan Sandler, executive director of

97

the Black Theatre Alliance, Mercedes Gregory, executive director of A Bunch of Experimental Theatres, and Robert Whitehead, the producer, significantly broadened the base of representation.

T. Edward Hambleton was elected as the first President of FACT at the meeting of December 6, 1974, and Dr. William J. Baumol as secretary-treasurer. In April, 1975, the executive director of FACT was appointed. He is Richard Kirschner, former director of the Annenberg Center for Communications at the University of Pennsylvania in Philadelphia.

The board determined that the funding base for FACT should be as broadly representative as was the Congress and therefore should include the support of government at the Federal and state levels, foundations, and business. But the bulk of its income eventually would come from the theatre itself by means of a small self-imposed theatre levy based on a percentage of box-office receipts.

These decisions were taken to make FACT a workable, continuing reality and an organization strong enough to play an advocacy role for the whole of the theatre. In the immediate post-Congress period, FACT, the continuing entity, inherited the complex multiple functions of the Congress. By identifying the shared and non-competitive needs of the different groups for whom it would speak, FACT would foster the spirit of cooperation and common approach developed at Princeton. It would seek to follow up the leads and promising ideas developed in the panels and plenary sessions. It would work to strengthen and solidify the personal and institutional contacts developed during the conference and to translate into action the areas of clear agreement arrived at during the conference. In its advocacy role it would endeavor to compile and disseminate the data and information necessary to the long-range purposes of FACT.

The panels in Princeton revealed some of the means by which theatre can strengthen its position in the 1970's and suggested the outlines of a program for a continuing FACT.

Such a program calls for an examination of ways to build audience through more advanced marketing methods and through the cultivation of young audiences at school level.

It recognizes the need to maintain effective contact with government officials as public funding becomes an increasingly necessary source of theatre support from top to bottom.

It seeks to broaden the base of foundation support and discover new approaches to business as more and more corporations evidence a sense of public responsibility to the arts.

It acknowledges theatre's vital stake in the life of the cities and in the restoration and renewal of the urban centers in which theatre traditionally flourishes.

It will advance the case for theatre among the other arts competing for attention in the editorial rooms of newspapers, magazines, and television stations.

Before June, 1974, no one could be sure that a theatre conference, convened in a time of social change, artistic uncertainty, and severe economic strain, could be a success or even complete its work. FACT was an acknowledged success and did complete its work. It survived ideological and sectional quarrels, accommodated widely differing points of view, and opened up communications channels that never before existed within the theatre.

The challenge of the future is in how well FACT can take up the threads of suggested action, common purpose, and mutuality achieved in Princeton and weave them into a program that all parts of the theatre can freely and fully support. How this challenge is met will affect not only the organizers of FACT, the delegates and panelists who made the Congress a success, and their constituents, but also all who care about the cultural vitality of the country and support live theatre as a unique and essential expression of that vitality.

Delegates, Panelists, Special Guests

(Titles and affiliations as at the time of the Congress)

ALSWANG, Ralph & Betty
Theatre Planning, Inc.

ANDERSON, Robert
The Dramatists Guild

ANDREWS, Bert
FACT Photographer

AYERS, Stephen Guy
Executive Producer
Children's Theatre Co. of the
Minneapolis Society of Fine Arts

BALLET, Arthur H.
Director, Office for Advanced
   Drama Research

BARDEL, William G.
Lehman Brothers

BARNETT, Joan
FACT Staff

BARR, Richard
President
League of New York Theatres
   and Producers

BARTMAN, William
West Coast Theatre Company

BARTOW, Arthur
Administrative Director
Theatre of the Riverside Church

BASINI, Richard
Community Consultant
Office of Midtown Planning
   and Development, New York

BAUMOL, Dr. William J.
Princeton University

BEADLE, Spofford
Producing Managers Company

BECK, Julian
The Living Theatre

BELL, Janet
Virginia Museum Theatre
   Repertory Co.

BENEDICT, Stephen
President, Theatre Development
   Fund

BERKOWSKY, Paul B.
Vice-President
League of Off-Broadway
   Theatres and Producers

BIRSH, Arthur
Publisher, Playbill

BISHOP, David
Managing Director
Alliance Theatre Company,
Atlanta, Georgia

BLISS, Anthony
Chairman, National Corporate
    Fund for the Dance

BOOTH, John E.
Associate Director
Twentieth Century Fund

BRIANT, Fredda
Business Representative
Theatrical Wardrobe Attendants
    Union Local 764

BRUSTAD, Wesley O.
Vice President
The Guthrie Theatre
    Foundation

BRUSTEIN, Robert
Dean, Yale School of Drama

BRYANT, Hazel Joan
Executive Director
Afro/American Total Theatre
    Arts Foundation

BUZBEE, Robert J.
Director of Civic Affairs
Sears, Roebuck & Co.

CARO, Warren
Director of Theatre Operations
The Shubert Organization

CHAPIN, Louis
Christian Science Monitor

CHAPIN, Schuyler G.
General Manager
Metropolitan Opera Association

CHERIN, Mrs. Miriam M.
Administrative Director
The Vanguard Theatre
    Pittsburgh, Pa.

CHERNACK, Peter Allen
Executive Director
The Company Theatre Foundation
Los Angeles, Calif.

CHESKIN, Irving W.
Executive Director
The League of N.Y. Theatres
    & Producers

CISNEY, Marcella
Director

CLURMAN, Richard M.
Chairman of the Board
City Center of Music and Drama

COHEN, Alexander H.
Producer

COHEN, William Court
Chairman of the Board
Theatre Now, Inc.

COIGNEY, Martha Wadsworth
Director
International Theatre Institute
    of the U.S.

CONKLIN, Senator William T.
Deputy Majority Leader
New York State Senate

CRAWFORD, Robert W.
President
Springhill Conference Center,
Wayzata, Minn.

CROUSE, Anna
Vice President
The Theatre Development Fund

CROYDEN, Margaret
Writer

DAVID, Michael
General Manager
Chelsea Theatre Center

DAVIDSON, Gordon
Artistic Director
Mark Taper Forum
Center Theatre Group

DEBUSKEY, Merle
President
Association of Theatrical
  Press Agents and Managers

DOERFLINGER, William H.
Manager
The Playhouse Theatre,
Wilmington, Del.

DuBROCK, Neal
Executive Producer
The Studio Arena Theatre
Buffalo, N.Y.

ECONOMOS, John
Managing Director
Goodman Theatre Center,
Chicago, Ill.

EDWARDS, Ben
President United Scenic Artists
  of America, Local 829

ERSKINE, Howard
Regional Manager, Ticketron

ERTAG, Nancy
Picket Productions

FEIST, Gene
Producing Director
The Roundabout Theatre

FELSER, Marcelle
Artistic Director
The Vanguard Theatre,
Pittsburgh, Pa.

FICHANDLER, Thomas
Executive Director
Arena Stage, Washington, D.C.

FISHER, Jules
Theatre Consultant

FISHKO, Robert
President
Council of Stock Theatres Inc.

FOWLER, Keith
Producing Director
Virginia Museum Repertory
  Company

FOX, Maxine
Producer

FRANK, David
Managing Director
Loretto-Hilton Repertory Theatre
St. Louis, Mo.

FRIED, Michael
Executive Director
The Roundabout Theatre

GALUSHA, Emily
Program Associate
Bush Foundation

GAYDOS, Linda
FACT Staff

GERSTEN, Bernard
Associate Producer
New York Shakespeare
  Festival

GILDER, Rosamond
President
International Theatre Institute
  of the U.S.

GISTER, Earle R.
Head, Drama Department
Carnegie-Mellon University

GLUECK, Grace
Cultural News Reporter
The New York Times

GOLODNER, Jack
President, J. Golodner Associates

GOOSEN, Larry
Administrative Director
Theatre at Saint Clement's

GRACEY, Janet
Theatre Development Fund

GRAHAM, Earl J.
Graham Agency

GREEN, Ruth
Assistant Executive Director
The League of N.Y. Theatres
  & Producers

GREGORY, Andre
Artistic Director
The Manhattan Project

GREGORY, Mercedes
Executive Director
A Bunch of Experimental
  Theatres of N.Y.

GRODY, Donald
Executive Secretary
Actors' Equity Association

GROSS, Jesse
Administrator
Theatre Guild-American
  Theatre Society

GROSS, Lynn
Producer
New York University
  School of the Arts

GROSS, Shelly
Music Fair Enterprises, Inc.

GRYNASTYL, Margaret
New York State Council
  on the Arts

GUBER, Lee
Music Fair Enterprises, Inc.

GUSSOW, Mel
The New York Times

HAMBLETON, T. Edward
Managing Director
The Phoenix Theatre

HARDY, Hugh
Hardy, Holzman, Pfeiffer
  Associates

HARNICK, Jay
Artistic Director
Performing Arts Repertory
  Theatre Foundation, Inc.

HAYS, Stephen E.
Managing Director
Stage West, West Springfield,
  Mass.

HEBSON, Pamela
American Express Card Division

HENRY, Patrick
Artistic Director
Free Street Theatre, Chicago, Ill.

HERSCHER, Seymour
Administrator, FACT

HERSCHER, Sylvia
Head, Theatre Department
E.H. Morris Company, Inc.

HEWES, Henry
Executive Secretary
American Theatre Planning
  Board

HORN, Barbara Lee
Producer

HORNER, Richard
Vice President
Coronet Theatre Corporation

HOUGHTON, Norris
Dean, Division of Theatre Arts
State University of New York
College at Purchase

HUGHES, Julie
FACT Staff

HUMMLER, Richard
FACT Staff

IZENOUR, George C.
Professor, Yale University

JACOBS, Bernard B.
Executive Director
Shubert Organization

JAFFE, Alan
Attorney, Proskauer, Rose,
  Goetz & Mendlesohn

JAVITS, Senator Jacob K.

JORDAN, Glenn
Executive Producer
Los Angeles Civic Light
  Opera Association

JORY, Jon
Producing Director
Actors Theatre of Louisville

KAHN, Virginia
Executive Director
Off Off Broadway Alliance

KALEM, Theodore E.
Drama Critic, Time Magazine

KEAN, Norman
President, Edison Theatre
  Corporation

KIMBALL, Steven Scott
Executive Secretary
The Stuart Ostrow Foundation

KING, Woodie, Jr.
Director, Henry Street
  Settlement New Federal
  Theatre

KIRSCHNER, Richard
Managing Director
Annenberg Center
University of Pennsylvania

KLEIN, Howard
Director for Arts
The Rockefeller Foundation

KLEIN, Stewart
Arts Editor, WNEW-TV

KOCH, Congressman Edward I.

KOONSMAN, Michael
Institutional Program Director
Hospital Audiences, Inc.

KRAWITZ, Herman
Consultant to the Arts

KROLL, Jack
Senior Editor & Drama Critic
Newsweek Magazine

LEACH, Robert H.
Vice President, Marketing
  Services
American Express Card Division

LEE, Ronald S.
Managing Officer, Theatre Party
  Associates

LEHMAN, Orin
President, Picket Productions,
  Inc.

LEVENSTEIN, Mary Kerney
Director, Circle in the Square
  Theatre School and Workshop

LeVINE, David E.
Executive Secretary
The Dramatists Guild

LEVINE, Johnna
Program Attorney
American Broadcasting Company

LIBIN, Paul
President, League of
  Off-Broadway Theatres &
  Producers

LICHTENSTEIN, Harvey
Executive Director
The Brooklyn Academy of Music

LLOYD, Lewis L.
Program Director, Performing
  Arts
New York State Council on the
  Arts

LONGACRE, Jay K.
Dir. of Management &
   Development
Studio Arena Theatre,
Buffalo, N.Y.

LOWRY, W. McNeil
Vice President, Division of
   Humanities and the Arts
The Ford Foundation

MALINA, Judith
The Living Theatre

MALLOW, Thomas W.
President
American Theatre Productions,
   Inc.

MANN, Ted
Artistic Director
Circle in the Square

MARKUS, Thomas B.
Artistic Director
Temple University
School of Communications
   and Theatre

MARRON, A. Vincent
Consultant
The Theatre Development Fund

MARTIN, Elliot
Producer

MASON, Marshall W.
Circle Repertory Theatre

MATTHAEI, Konrad
Theatre Owner/Producer

MATTHEWS, Hale

MAXWELL, Douglas
Studio Arena Theatre
Buffalo, N.Y.

MAYLEAS, Ruth
Director of Theatre Programs
National Endowment for the Arts

MAZZOLA, John W.
Managing Director
Lincoln Center for the
   Performing Arts

McCANN, Elizabeth
Managing Director
Nederlander Productions

McCLELLAND, Maurice
International Theatre Institute
   of the U.S.

McGAHA, James
Trustee, Union Executive Board
Wardrobe Attendants
   Union Local 764

McKENZIE, James B.
Executive Producer
The American Conservatory
   Theatre

MEADOW, Lynne
Artistic Director
The Manhattan Theatre Club

MERRICK, David
Producer

MILLER, Michael J.
President
League of Professional Theatre
Training Programs, Inc.

MINSKOFF, Jerome
Minskoff Theatre

MITTELMAN, Arnold
The Whole Theatre Company,
Montclair, N.J.

MORDECAI, Benjamin
Producing Director
Indiana Repertory Theatre, Inc.

MORISON, Bradley G.
Theatre Consultant

MORRELL, Jesse
Community Relations Director
Free Southern Theatre

MORRISON, Hobe and Toni
Variety

MOSES, Gilbert
Director

MOSS, Robert
Executive Producer
Playwrights Horizons

MUNK, Erika
Performance Magazine

MURPHY, Thomas
Theatre Development Fund

NARAMORE, Elaine
Executive Director
New York Cultural Council

NICHTERN, Claire
Producer

NUSSBAUM, Jeremy
Greenbaum, Wolff & Ernst

O'CONNOR, Kevin
Artistic Director
Theatre at Saint Clement's

OLSEN, Kenneth M.
President
Columbia Artists Theatricals,
  Corp.
Columbia Artists
  Management, Inc.

OPPER, Barry
Administrative Director
ProVisional Theatre,
Los Angeles, Calif.

PAPP, Joseph
New York Shakespeare Festival

PARKS, Hildy
Writer/Producer

PAS, Leonard, Jr.
Director, Division of
  Cultural Affairs,
Department of State,
Tallahassee, Florida

PAYNE, David W.
Deputy Director
Performing Arts Program
New York State Council
  on the Arts

PINERO, Miguel
Playwright

PRICE, Lorin E.
Producer

RADLER, Carl
President
Metropolitan Ticket Agents
  Guild

RICHARDS, Lloyd
President
Society of Stage Directors
  and Choreographers

ROBERTS, Louise
Director, Clark Center

ROBERTS, Vera Mowry
Chairman, Theatre &
  Cinema Department, Hunter
  College

ROBINSON, Janet
Managing Officer
Theatre Party Associates

RUBIN, Joan A.
Editor-in-Chief, Playbill

SABBS, Darrell
Black Repertory Theatre

SABINSON, Harvey & Sarah
Consultant to the Arts

SANDLER, Joan
Executive Director
Black Theatre Alliance

SAYAD, Homer
Haskins & Sells

SCHECHNER, Richard
Co-Director
The Performance Group

SCHEEDER, Louis W.
Producer, Folger Theatre Group

SCHIER, Ernest
The Evening/Sunday Bulletin
Philadelphia, Pa.

SCHMIDT, Sandra
Los Angeles Times

SCHNITZER, Robert C.
Executive Director
University Resident Theatre
    Assoc.

SCHOENBAUM, Donald
Managing Director
The Guthrie Theatre

SCHOENFELD, Gerald
Executive Director
The Shubert Organization

SCOTT, Harold
Artistic Director
Cincinnati Playhouse in the Park

SEPTEE, Moe & Ruth
The New Locust Theatre
Philadelphia, Pa.

SHAKTMAN, Ben
Director

SIFF, Iris
Alley Theatre

SOLMSSEN, Peter
Advisor on the Arts
Department of State
Bureau of Educational &
    Cultural Affairs

SOMLYO, Roy A.
General Manager
Alexander H. Cohen

SOUTHERN, Hugh
Executive Director
Theatre Development Fund

SPENCER, Michael Jon
Executive Director
Hospital Audiences, Inc.

STASIO, Marilyn
Drama Critic, Cue Magazine

STERN, Alfred
Consultant to FACT

STEVENSON, Isabelle
President, The American
    Theatre Wing

STEWART, William
Managing Director
American Shakespeare Theatre

STORCH, Arthur
Artistic Director
Syracuse Stage

STRAIGHT, Michael
National Endowment for the
    Arts

SWIRE, Willard E.
Vice President
Theatre Authority, Inc.

THORN, George
Eugene O'Neill Memorial
    Theatre Center

ULMER, John
Stage West
West Springfield, Mass.

USTINOV, Peter & Helene

VALDEZ, Luis
El Centro Campesino Cultural

VENZA, Jac
Director of Performance
  Programs
WNET/13

WAISSMAN, Kenneth
Producer

WALKER, Hugh
President & General Manager
O'Keefe Center for the
  Performing Arts

WARD, Douglas Turner
Artistic Director
Negro Ensemble Company

WEAVER, Richard
Secretary-Treasurer
Assoc. of Theatrical Press Agents
  and Managers

WEIDNER, Paul
Producing Director
Hartford Stage Company

WEINSTEIN, Richard
Consultant
Rockefeller Brothers Fund

WHITE, George C.
President, Eugene O'Neill
  Memorial Theatre Center

WILSON, Edwin
Wall Street Journal

WOLSK, Eugene V.
Wolsk & Azenberg

WOOD, Audrey
Head of Play Department
International Famous Agency

WOODMAN, Elizabeth Roberts
Casting Director
Goodman Theatre Center

WOODMAN, William
Artistic Director
Goodman Theatre

YOUNGBLOOD, Harold
Director of Special Programs
New York State Council
  on the Arts

ZALKEN, William & Bernice
General Manager
Municipal Opera, St. Louis, Mo.

ZEIGLER, Joseph Wesley
Vice President
Arts Development Associates

ZEISLER, Peter
Director, Theatre
  Communications Group

ZERBE, John B.
General Manager
Hershey Community Theatre
Hershey, Pa.

ZESCH, Lindy
Theatre Communications Group

Note on Author

Stuart W. Little, a journalist and editor, first became involved in the theatre when he began writing a theatre news column for the New York Herald Tribune in 1959. He is the author of *Enter Joseph Papp* (1974), *Off-Broadway* (1972), and *The Playmakers* (1970), with Arthur Cantor. He is the editor of The Authors Guild Bulletin, a director of the Theatre Development Fund, a trustee of the American-Scandinavian Foundation, and a member of the Play Selection Committee of the Theatre Guild-American Theatre Society.